SAVAGE MULES

SAVAGE MULES:

The Democrats and Endless War

DENNIS PERRIN

VERSO

London • New York

First published by Verso 2008
Copyright © Dennis Perrin, 2008

The moral rights of the authors and translators have been asserted

1 3 5 7 9 10 8 6 4 2

Verso
UK: 6 Meard Street, London W1F 0EG
USA: 180 Varick Street, New York, NY 10014-4606
www.versobooks.com

Verso is the imprint of New Left Books

ISBN: 978-1-84467-265-3

British Library Cataloguing in Publication Data
A catalogue record for this book is available from the British Library

Library of Congress Cataloging-in-Publication Data
A catalog record for this book is available from the Library of Congress

Typeset in Bembo by Hewer Text UK Ltd, Edinburgh
Printed in the USA by Maple Vail

HEE HAW

"We're not inflicting pain on these fuckers. When people kill us, they should be killed in greater numbers. I believe in killing people who try to hurt you. And I can't believe we're being pushed around by these two-bit pricks."

So riffed President Bill Clinton in 1993, reviewing his options in Somalia, according to former aide turned TV host George Stephanopoulos in his book *All Too Human*.

Not quite the dope-smoking, adulterous anti-American commie that many right-wingers believed, and still believe, Clinton to be. But in American politics, reality is elastic, and can be stretched to fit any ideological mindset. Lash out privately at enemies real and imagined, Nixon-style; bomb smaller countries; marginalize the poor; further erode the Constitution while strengthening the police state; serve elites who never have to run for public office to enforce their interests—but if you happen to be a

Democrat, you are immediately slimed as a "socialist" or worse by those who applaud and defend similar policies when enacted by Republicans.

This political fantasia is scarcely the sole property of the American right. Liberals have their own strange visions about US political reality. I've witnessed this up-close and point-blank for much of my adult life. To many of them, the Democrats are a flawed but inherently decent party whose humane outlook is forever compromised by Republican slanders and personal insecurity. Even critical liberal bloggers and columnists hand the Dems a pass on most issues, simply because they believe that the mules will eventually Get It Right, if only they can move past conservative lies and intimidation tactics.

Structural analysis is not a liberal Democratic trait.

But no matter. There are elections to be won, and many wrongs to be righted, whatever they may be, so American liberals must insist that the Democratic Party, if given enough power and positive reinforcement, will spread peace and prosperity to those who deserve it most: namely, American liberals who are active in the political arena. Their chief model for this? Bill Clinton, of course.

To say that the former president enjoys rock/porn-star status among American liberals is both obvious and an under-statement (diminished somewhat by his attacks on Barack Obama). For the past few years, Clinton's veep Al Gore has encroached on his former leader's turf, receiving plaudits and hosannas from liberals nationwide. Their weak-kneed, light-headed reaction to Gore winning the Nobel Peace Prize was truly a spectacle to witness, and had Gore then thrown himself into the presidential race, his political stock would have smashed through the roof. But it seemed that Gore had more sense than his swooning fans, who were left sobbing about lack of choices, and fantasized about a Gore administration that never was, but perhaps could be.

The Clinton/Gore years did a serious number on what remained of American liberalism. But in many ways that administration was true to much of the Democratic Party's history. From their first president—Andrew Jackson in 1828—to now, the Democrats have robbed, cheated, and lied to their constituents, while waging war on enemies, foreign and domestic, who threatened their power and means to make mega-profits. Hardly an earth-shattering statement, yes? But for a good many American liberals the above characterization is science fiction, if not open slander. They have convinced themselves that the better features of the Party—say, support for civil rights legislation, or legal abortion, or some kind of environmental protection—represent the true Democratic core, and that the uglier aspects are either deviations or cynical exercises in political expediency. This is why many liberal bloggers tolerate being kicked in the face time and time again. Sure, they don't like it, but if they can withstand the punishment, perhaps their abusive masters will reconsider

PIOUS MULES MAKE EFFECTIVE ASSASSINS

Poor Jimmy Carter.

Since the middle of his only term in office, Carter has been seen by most of the political mainstream as a washout, a disaster, an incumbent who inspired an intra-party challenge in 1980 from Ted Kennedy—which failed, but not before damaging Carter's re-election bid.

The American right believes that Carter has always been treasonous scum. Many American liberals didn't dare mention his name favorably until years after Carter left office, when he helped to build houses for low-income families. Jimmy Carter's presidency is considered a joke and a national disaster. Lesser men wouldn't dare show their faces in public after that, much less speak out on social issues.

The main problem with the Carter years is one of simple perception. After winning the 1976 election, Carter made a big fuss about how his administration would promote human rights around the world, in stark contrast to the

Nixon and Ford approaches to foreign policy. The reality was of course much different. Jimmy Carter politically supported and helped finance all manner of human rights abuses.

- Ignoring the pleas of Salvadoran Archbishop Oscar Romero, Carter pumped money and arms into the Salvadoran security forces that were responsible for the majority of bloodshed in that country, including the assassination of Romero himself.

- Carter replenished the Indonesian military with a steady supply of weapons as President Suharto continued massacring a sizable chunk of the East Timorese population.

- Carter and his high-level officials backed Gen. Chun Doo Hwan's military regime in South Korea, especially after the Kwangju massacre in 1980, when some 2,000 pro-democracy students were mowed down in the streets by the South Korean Special Forces.

- On Carter's watch, the most reactionary, violent elements in the Muslim world were recruited through Pakistan's Directorate for Inter-Services Intelligence (ISI) to fight the Soviet-backed regime in Afghanistan. This included assaults on women wearing Western clothes, and attacks on co-ed schools—a specialty of the then-unknown Osama bin Laden.

It was in Afghanistan that Carter drew his biggest line. In his final State of the Union Address, on January 23, 1980, Carter made it clear how he and the foreign policy elite viewed the recent Soviet invasion. Afghanistan was but the first communist step toward regional expansion, a geopolitical move intended to grab

> more than two-thirds of the world's exportable oil. The Soviet effort to dominate Afghanistan has brought Soviet military forces to within 300 miles of the Indian Ocean and close to the Straits of Hormuz, a waterway through which most of the world's oil must flow. The Soviet Union is now attempting to consolidate a strategic position, therefore, that poses a grave threat to the free movement of Middle East oil.

Carter then waved his dented saber:

> Let our position be absolutely clear: An attempt by any outside force to gain control of the Persian Gulf region will be regarded as an assault on the vital interests of the United States of America, and such an assault will be repelled by any means necessary, including military force.

Strong stuff. Indeed, that portion of Carter's speech wouldn't sound foreign in the mouths of Ronald Reagan or George W. Bush. And while he was seen as flaccid and ineffectual, Carter at least understood the Bigger Picture, and responded accordingly. The Persian Gulf region, with all that bubbling crude under sand, belonged to the United States, and there was simply no way that Carter could overlook any potential "outside force" taking what was rightfully ours.

Of course, part of Carter's tough tone stemmed from the recent hostage crisis in Iran, where Islamic militant students held fifty-two Americans captive, in protest against years of US meddling in Iran, primarily its support of the Shah. The hostage-taking on November 4, 1979 deepened Carter's public reputation for being a "soft" leader; and when the Soviets invaded Afghanistan just over a month later, it appeared as if the Carter administration was standing around, hands in pockets, allowing the nation's enemies to take advantage of its inertia.

In a sense, Jimmy Carter was given control of the American machine at a point when it was malfunctioning. Anxiety, anger, inflation, recession, imperial disillusionment, national malaise—all these and more he inherited. Plus the governing class and its stenographers were in a nasty mood, put off by the lingering influence of Sixties activism and feeling more anti-democratic than ever. A bleak political period. Too bad Ronald Reagan didn't snag the GOP nomination in 1976 and win the general election. He probably would have been Jimmy Carter instead.

Still, for those with a serious stake in the system, the Carter years did much to stabilize the imperial state, lending it the "human rights" cover that allowed mass murder and theft to continue apace, only at a different speed and under softer lights.

Some hubris remained.

Explaining why the US refused to offer Vietnam reparations for turning vast areas of that country into smoldering moonscape, slaughtering millions in the process, Carter said calmly that "the destruction was mutual." No significant eyebrows were raised. No derisive laughter emanated from the stenographers' pool. Vietnam apparently hit us as hard as we hit them—maybe harder. Tough to tell amid the smoking ruins of New York and DC. But only a Democrat could utter that line and get away with it. It would sound too harsh coming from a Republican. Again, Jimmy Carter smoothed over some rocky years, providing a transition to a re-energized, boastful imperial period.

Carter never received the credit due to him for being president under such shitty circumstances. That he later hammered nails for the poor and made some critical sounds about Israeli occupation takes nothing away from his service to the war state. He remains America's most underrated imperialist.

MULE SHIT ON THE SOFA

But let's not pile on Jimmy Carter. He's hardly the worst specimen of Warrior Dem, nor was he outside the general, elite consensus. Simply put, the Democrats will never undermine a system that gave them life and has nourished them ever since. It's been all downhill since the Louisiana Purchase. Indeed, it's somewhat perplexing that liberals, when mocked as "weak" by American reactionaries, don't point to their Party's long, bloody history of territorial expansion and military aggression.

The stirring phrase "Manifest Destiny" is a Dem original. Andrew Jackson was a dedicated, accomplished ethnic cleanser—a Milosevic with better hair—forcibly relocating anywhere from 45,000 to 70,000 Indians while in office. Martin Van Buren picked up Jackson's cue, overseeing, among other crimes, the Trail of Tears, killing some 4,000 Cherokee. And James Polk? Thanks to his war on Mexico ("a war unnecessarily and unconstitutionally begun by the President of the United States" as a Congressional rebuke at the time put it, with Rep Abe Lincoln in support), the remainder of the continental United States filled out, making room for freeways, strip malls, Hollywood, Vegas, celebrity-studded desert golf tournaments, and Napa Valley vineyard tours.

To be fair, a number of Dem defeatists appeared as the US entered middle age. Many of them were "Copperheads," opposed the Civil War on the grounds that it was ruinous, pointless, and served to strengthen the dictatorial power of President Lincoln. Much of their opposition was based on racism, hatred of abolitionists, concern for dwindling markets, and a fear of a consolidated US. Needless to say, the Copperheads bet on the wrong greyhound. This turn against a major American war was somewhat of a first for Democrats (though there were those who backed Lincoln)—a position that a portion of the Party would thereafter take, for various reasons other than the white-skin privilege of the Copperheads. Once the US was solidified and planned to expand even further, the mainstream of the Dems went along with the imperial consensus, when not shaping this consensus themselves.

There's little chance that today's liberals would look to the Copperheads for guidance. Still, there are points of comparison, primarily in each generation's absolute loathing of its President, on the grounds that the Chief Exec. was a war-mongering tyrant. The Copperheads were much more violent in their anti-administration rhetoric, however, openly calling for the overthrow of the government, at times advocating Lincoln's assassination. To the Starbucks/laptop Dems, such hostility would be considered counterproductive, as it might hurt the Party's chances in the next midterms.

Perhaps the best example of Democratic muscle-flexing is that of Woodrow Wilson's administration (1913–21). Throughout his first term, Wilson invaded and occupied Mexico, the Dominican Republic, Haiti, and Nicaragua— regional targets that were considered US property, or at least lacking autonomy worthy of American respect. But Wilson's most ambitious military foray came at the start of his second term, in 1917, when, after campaigning against US entry into the European war, Wilson immediately made plans to enter the European war. German submarine warfare in the Atlantic certainly helped Wilson's cause (even though the US was shipping arms to Germany's enemies), but it was clear long before that the Anglophile president would eventually side with Britain and France in containing a burgeoning Germany, which wanted its cut of global capital action.

Once Wilson got rolling, the nation became his private preserve.

Unable to convince enough young men to voluntarily

enter his meat-grinder for democracy, Wilson instituted
a military draft. And to make sure that no antiwar radicals
fucked with his grand plan, Wilson oversaw the passage
of the Espionage Act in June 1917, following it a year
later with the Sedition Act. Under Woodrow Wilson, it
became a federal crime to oppose the war openly, or
denounce the state itself. This stemmed partly from the
need to intimidate American youth into joining the mass
slaughter overseas; but much of Wilson's reasoning was
in reaction to the rise of political militancy, led by
American radicals.

Few liberals like being criticized from their left, as it
tends to expose them for who they really are. In Wilson's
case, it was a matter of geopolitical positioning, lucrative
foreign markets, a much-needed stimulus to the sagging
national economy (war is the state's best friend, etc.), and
domestic political and social control. When radical newspapers and magazines lost their mailing rights, which
essentially killed their circulations, it helped Wilson, given
how accurately they had portrayed him to the masses.
But in order to send a serious message to those who
opposed him, Wilson found a flesh-and-blood figure to
whip publicly—Eugene Victor Debs.

Every American schoolchild knows Debs' story.
[EDITOR'S NOTE: Is that true? ME: Are you drunk?
I tossed that in for narrative flow. EDITOR AGAIN:
Oh jeez. Right. Sorry.] A populist orator from Terre

Haute, Indiana who became a national socialist phenom-
enon, Debs drew large crowds and regaled them with
passionate political speeches, humane appeals, and
sardonic humor. When Wilson cranked up the US war
machine, Debs was perhaps his most prominent,
eloquent, effective critic. That the criticism came from
Wilson's left may or may not have meant anything to
the imperial president, but as any decent pro-war liberal
understands, why deal with it at all? So, to the cheers
of his liberal supporters, and backed by liberal Supreme
Court justices like Oliver Wendell Holmes, Wilson had
Debs arrested for violating his war decrees, throwing
him into prison in 1919, after some 50,000 Americans
had been blown apart in France and "democracy"
secured.

This wasn't the first time Debs had seen the slammer.
During the Pullman Strike of 1894, Debs spoke out in
favor of the railroad workers, violating a federal injunction
to end the strike. Debs was arrested and spent six months
in prison, while federal troops were called in to smash
the Pullman strikers. And who was the president that
ordered this military assault on political speech and militant
action within the United States? Why, Grover Cleveland,
of course. A Democrat.

Sentenced to ten years under Wilson, Debs served
just over two, his sentence commuted in 1921 by Warren
Harding—a Republican. But jailing Debs was only a

small part of Wilson's domestic repression. Working with Attorney General A. Mitchell Palmer, Wilson's administration went after not only those who opposed the war, but—most aggressively—those who opposed the system itself.

Wilson had plenty of help and sympathy, from newspaper editors to police captains to local Party machines and various "pro-American" vigilante groups, as his administration turned the war on its domestic enemies— socialists and anarchists mostly, tarred in the press as "Reds" and "Bolsheviks," but also feminists, pacifists, and radical immigrants, those who chose to keep a hyphen in their names, "who have poured the poison of disloyalty into the very arteries of our national life; who have sought to bring the authority and good name of our Government into contempt," and therefore "must be crushed out," as Wilson put it in his 1915 State of the Union address. By the end of Wilson's second term, this crushing had proved largely successful, thanks to routine violations of the First and Fourth Amendments, and to physical deportations. To this day, Woodrow Wilson is revered and respected by smart, influential people who understand that political challenges to their privilege and power must be thwarted, if not destroyed, depending on the urgency of the moment.

Wilson helped to create the modern American police

state. Both major parties have since refined and improved the original model, but it took a Democrat to reveal the possibilities of serious state repression. Another mule-kick to the national skull.

HOOFPRINTS

While writing the very book you're now holding, I was asked by several people why I chose the moniker "mules" to describe Democrats. Isn't their mascot a donkey? And aren't there many differences between donkeys and mules?

Technically, yes, if you want to get literal about it. But "donkeys" sounds too cumbersome, while "mules" is tighter, sharper, and suggests a certain stubbornness that is decidedly present in a great number of American liberals looking to justify their Dem worship, even when they concede that their representatives screw them. "Donkeys" doesn't adequately cover this: it's too playful a noun, Eddie Murphy cracking wise in *Shrek*. I suppose I could've gone with "Savage Zebroids," a mix of zebra and any other equid, but that's more sci-fi in tone, and would attract an audience expecting galactic battles and exploding planets—not that Dems wouldn't support such things. Perhaps in the next book.

The Democrats' symbol can be traced back to Andrew Jackson's first campaign, when Sharp Knife, as the Cherokee knowingly named him, was called a "jackass" by his opponents. Jackson embraced the word and flaunted the donkey image throughout his presidential run. But it wasn't until Thomas Nast, the influential nineteenth-century political cartoonist, portrayed the Democrats as donkeys in *Harper's Weekly* in 1874 (while also establishing Republicans as elephants) that the symbol permanently stuck. Still, given the staggering levels of bloodshed unleashed by Democrats since their inception, a donkey is hardly the proper anthropomorphic beast to convey the Party's true identity. A donkey with a cruise missile, maybe, but those things are pretty heavy, and would eventually weaken the animal and cause its collapse.

A tiger shark would make a better mascot, as would a hawk, a wolf, or a crocodile. Yet to really capture the essence of the Democrats over time, one must look to the insect world. While the fire ant is highly aggressive and somewhat toxic, thus a fitting symbol, I'd have to go with the praying mantis. Its praying posture would appeal to a broad religious base; its features resemble white-collar, liberal wonks, a key demographic; it will kill just about any creature it can subdue, whether insect, bird, amphibian, reptile, or mammal, which takes care of the toughness issue; and most importantly, the praying mantis kills and eats its own, a well-renowned Democratic trait.

Imagine a Democratic convention where the delegates don giant mantis heads, nodding and vibrating in unison as their Party's candidate lays down the Good Word from the illuminated dais. "We will rip out the Republicans' throats, then devour them from the feet up as they helplessly look on, dying in our mandibles. Can I get a 'No Mercy!'"

"NO MERCY!"

Savage Mantises. Run against *that*, pachyderms.

MULE DEAL UNDONE

Much of modern liberals' confusion about the true nature of their Party originates in the New Deal.

From 1921 to 1933, the Republicans, overseeing increasing income inequality, bad central bank policies, bad banking regulations, and gold standard trade wars, had helped to run the US economy into the dirt. By the time Franklin Delano Roosevelt returned the presidency to the Democrats, the nation was in a serious economic hole, and FDR was willing to experiment with the role of the federal government—in his case, expanding the national state in order to boost employment, protect vulnerable citizens (social security for the old), and generally reinvigorate the depressed economy by making the government a partner in business operations.

Of course, many leading business organizations and figures were appalled by such federal intrusion into the "free market," suggesting that perhaps Roosevelt, a son of privilege, was an emerging-from-the-closet socialist. Conservative Democrats opposed FDR's expansion— especially Southern mules, who feared that the New Deal would give their African-American population crazy ideas about political and social equality. They needn't have worried. While Roosevelt wasn't particularly pro-segregation, neither was he a civil rights dynamo, refusing to make lynching a federal crime, nor looking to oppose the poll tax, which kept Southern blacks essentially voiceless in local elections. Even within New Deal programs there was racial discrimination, as whites received more pay than blacks—if a jobs program even hired African-Americans in the first place.

Still, FDR set in motion forces that would eventually inspire more democratic activism domestically. And for that, he and his wife Eleanor, who was considered the real progressive force behind the throne, were revered by scores of American liberals. However, FDR's political plans went far beyond reordering the national scene: there was a rising global empire to help build and guide. This naturally meant aggressive moves financially, which in time would fully blossom in a devastating global war.

Two chief areas that the Roosevelt administration and its elite economic backers were seriously keen on were the oil reserves in the Middle East, and lucrative markets throughout Asia, the southeast portion of which also possessed oil. In the former, the imperial British were on the way out, clearing the way for an American corporate presence, its representatives courting the ruling families of Saudi Arabia. In the latter there was a huge and growing obstacle—namely, Japanese imperial expansion and military occupation. This was seen as a pressing problem, since the Japanese appeared unaware that Asian markets and material resources belonged to US business interests and their global allies, primarily the British.

The war with Japan began long before Pearl Harbor, and had unfolded as FDR settled in for his extended White House stay. Japan's brutal occupation of China led to calls for a quarantine, most vocally by Henry Luce, who sided with Chinese nationalists in an effort to Christianize that country. But it wasn't until the Japanese moved into Indochina that the real fun began. The US and Britain slapped an oil embargo on Japan, which was widely considered on all sides as an aggressive act, if not an act of war. While there was a brief split within the Japanese elite about whether to fight the US or negotiate a Japanese withdrawal in exchange for a loosening of the embargo, it was clear that FDR's actions would not be seriously reversed, and that negotiation was largely a pantomime; so Japan's hawks planned the attack that would pull the United States into the mass killing already underway, believing that the conflict would be a brief one at worst.

After Pearl Harbor, the US went into total war-state mode, not only on the military front, but, more importantly, on the economic front as well. As Woodrow Wilson had discovered, there's nothing like massive military spending to juice an economy, and having a foreign enemy helps to divert attention away from the machinations of state, focusing the nation on a single, sinister figure, which the mass media can inflate and refine.

In the far bloodier sequel to Wilson's war, FDR had three sinister figures to feed his domestic population: Tojo, Mussolini, and Hitler. That all three were murderous tyrants made it much easier to rally the nation (even though, in the years before Pearl Harbor, Mussolini and Hitler had been admired by influential segments of the US corporate class, from Ford to DuPont to Texaco to IBM, partly for their anti-union policies, partly as a bulwark against Soviet communism, but mostly due to the fact—especially in Hitler's case—that these and other companies had made a lot of money under their rule). But with the Japanese, there was the racial angle to exploit, and Roosevelt's government encouraged slimy, buck-toothed "Jap" caricatures throughout the popular culture.

It wasn't enough to depict the overseas Japanese as crazed insects and snakes trying to devour the world; Roosevelt decided to wage war on the domestic Japanese population as well, a large number of whom were American citizens. To this day, there are people who remain shocked and dismayed over the mass incarceration of Japanese-Americans (though many contemporary right-wingers see nothing wrong with it, and wish that Arab-Americans could meet the same fate). But really, is it that surprising, considering the tenor of that time? And does it seriously stun anyone that a "liberal" like FDR oversaw such a policy? As we have seen, and will further discover, American liberals can be, and often have been, as authoritarian and brutal as those they deem politically dangerous. Rounding up civilians and throwing them into camps is nothing to the liberal imagination. Indeed, it may be one of liberalism's more benevolent traits.

Unlike Wilson's war, to which there was a significant domestic opposition, FDR's entry into the Second World War enjoyed massive support across the political terrain. Those who protested were mostly pacifists, isolationists, and a smattering of socialists, who insisted (not completely incorrectly) that the Second World War was yet another conflict between competing imperialist powers, only much more destructive, with a higher body count. There were some 42,000 conscientious objectors against that slaughter (more than during the First World War); those who refused alternative service or didn't register for the draft—about 6,000 men overall—were sent to prison.

No matter. The wars in Europe and Asia—the first an outgrowth of Germany's defeat in 1918 and subsequent humiliation and punishment, the second a geopolitical

BLOOD IN THE MULE'S MOUTH

As Roosevelt wasted away in the final days of the Second World War, his vice president, Harry Truman, prepared to assume command, and bring the Pacific theater to a thunderous close.

Japanese imperialism lay in ruins. It was clear, save to the ideologically blind, that Japan's attempt to control Asia and dominate its markets had failed. Once Truman was sworn into office and briefed on the Manhattan Project, Give 'em Hell Harry knew he held the ultimate trump card, calling on Japanese leaders to surrender completely and unconditionally—no compromises, no extended deals.

Japan dragged its feet, its hardliners calling for a final, balls-to-the-wall battle, sacrificing millions of its own citizens if necessary. Anything to inflict whatever pain they could on the Americans before the inevitable end. Last-minute efforts to persuade the Soviets to help broker a more favorable truce came to nothing. (In fact, the Soviets soon declared war on Japan, invading Manchuria.) So while Japanese elites argued among themselves about how best to proceed, Truman gave the order to destroy Hiroshima.

August 6, 1945—together with August 9, when Nagasaki was introduced to the atomic bomb—became a unique chapter in the history of Democratic slaughter. While it took additional, conventional firebombing of other Japanese targets to bring the war truly to an end, the unleashing of nuclear weapons, with the specter of more, savagely sealed the deal. Not only was this the ultimate triumph of American military might and technology; it showed to the world that the US would not hesitate to destroy anyone who got in the way of its global interests. An old empire was brutally replaced with an emerging, much stronger one. Just as the good Lord intended.

There is concern in some quarters that today's American youth aren't being taught to appreciate—even to admire—Truman's nuclear assault. Relativist thinking might undermine support for the war state, frightening those charged with stirring patriotic emotion. My generation had no such worries. We were taught that the nuking of Japan was a boon to modern civilization, and that Harry Truman was one of the more decisive, humanitarian presidents in US history.

My first exposure to Hiroshima and Nagasaki came in sixth grade, in Mr Eschenbraun's social studies class. The thirty-something, blond, crew-cut teacher made the nukings seem almost mystical—not only a miracle of American ingenuity, but also of masculine resolve and guts, traits that the rest of the world respected and feared. Now, Mr Eschenbraun spoke this way about most US wars we studied, including Vietnam, which was then still raging. In fact, he would go off on tangents about dirty hippies and draft-dodgers, stating that if any peace creeps tried passive resistance in front of his car, he would run over them without a care, perhaps backing up and doing it again for flag and country. Roasting the Japs? No-brainer.

I don't recall any parents protesting at Mr Eschenbraun's academic approach. Mine certainly didn't. It was a simpler time.

Despite fears that Truman's bombings may have lost their luster, many present-day liberals celebrate the only use (so far) of nuclear weapons on civilian targets—a big reason being that a Democratic president did the honors. This shows, retrospectively, that liberals can mass murder minus second thoughts. No objective reader of history would ever doubt the liberal love of violence and destruction; but the right-wing media machine has so effectively portrayed liberals as wimps and traitors that Truman's order becomes a handy counter-argument.

The nuking of Hiroshima and Nagasaki (the latter of which endured winds up to 1,000 mph, and a ground temperature of 9,000 degrees) was celebrated in its day as well, but this didn't ensure that Truman would glide to victory in 1948. The 1946 midterms handed the House and Senate to the GOP, and there were defections inside the Democratic Party itself. By 1948, Southern segregationists split from the Dems, nominating Strom Thurmond as their presidential candidate. The left got behind FDR's former vice president, Henry Wallace, whom Truman had fired from his cabinet for having alleged pro-Soviet sympathies. The Republicans, lacking the spirit and imagination displayed by the Democrats, served up their 1944 nominee, Thomas Dewey, for a second run. As he had against an ailing Roosevelt, Dewey lost to a more robust Truman—despite the *Chicago Daily Tribune*'s infamous election-night headline: "Dewey Defeats Truman."

Having secured a four-year term of his own, Truman sought to expand his self-named Doctrine, announced in 1947. While Woodrow Wilson and FDR oversaw the militarization of their respective political periods, it was Truman who took the concept to the next, inevitable level: the National Security State. Alarmed by rebellion in Greece and possible Soviet moves against Turkey, Truman pumped money and arms into the two countries, looking to cement ties with the ruling circles of each state.

Depicted domestically as "defense" against communism, Truman's policy was in fact an aggressive attempt to widen the US global sphere. In Turkey, Truman found a willing recipient for all that Washington had to offer, which in turn gave the US a friendly frontline state against the Soviet Union. In Greece, Truman backed right-wing militarists attempting to suppress the main guerrilla army that had resisted the Nazi occupation. The Greek royalists were given advanced weaponry, including napalm, and were assisted by US military advisers. By 1949, the anti-royalist resistance was vanquished, and Greece succumbed to a military dictatorship friendly to Western business interests, buoyed by the Marshall Plan.

Through the Marshall Plan, Truman and his advisers sought to rebuild war-ravaged Europe into a vital economic force, to complement and be dominated by US corporate power. The Plan was also meant to isolate the Soviets, who showed an early interest in Truman's policy, but weren't seriously considered by the West as an economic partner. The US was interested solely in global dominance, and the Soviet Union, soon followed by Mao's China, were large, annoying obstacles to this arrangement. In order to ensure that the American population went along with the official narrative, Truman turned his war inward, employing loyalty oaths, domestic spying, and massive state propaganda to secure compliance. Like Wilson's Espionage and Sedition acts, and FDR's

Smith Act, Truman's authoritarian ploy was accepted and applauded by many mainstream liberals.

Still, fighting the Other through foreign clients can keep people obedient for only so long. Another war in which American troops were actively involved would doubtless help keep the domestic population in line, if the recent European and Pacific killing grounds were any guide.

Trouble in Korea seemed the perfect remedy.

After enduring thirty-five years of Japanese occupation, Korea fell under foreign occupation again, from the Soviets in the North and the US in the South. Not surprisingly, each sphere reflected the features of its occupier: tensions exacerbated by years of internecine political fighting, class conflicts, competing socioeconomic models, and related human pleasures. By 1949, civil war appeared inevitable, each side skirmishing with the other, until, in 1950, the North took it to the next level, sweeping into the South and causing all hell to break loose.

The timing couldn't have been better for Truman. His war on domestic enemies took on a global dimension, making it seem as if the US was fighting for its life both at home and abroad. The liberal intelligentsia played its role, fleshing out a larger narrative whereby commie power-grabs were resisted by the scrappy, determined, freedom-loving West.

Reality differed.

As in Greece, the US backed and armed combatants

in Korea who had collaborated with their Axis occupiers—
though, at the time, this was not highlighted at home.
After years of racist, anti-Japanese rhetoric, how would
it look if America suddenly helped those who had fought
on behalf of the Rising Sun? Instead, the bug-eyed beasts
were now Korean communists, even though they had
been on the Allied side during the war. One might think
that such a swift, propagandistic turnaround would be
tough to sell; but the American talent for self-delusion
and desire to believe in New Truths should never be
underestimated. The US didn't fight the Asian war in
order simply to hand the region's resources to local nationalists—especially if those nationalists marched under the
hammer and sickle. So, for the second time in less than
a decade, the US, led by a Democratic president, aimed
its big guns east.

As a kid in school, I didn't learn a lot about the Korean
war. It wasn't taught as extensively as the Revolutionary
and Civil wars, much less the Second World War. But
then, this was during the Vietnam War, which seemed
bigger and more damaging than anything seen in Korea,
so that might have pushed the earlier conflict off the
curriculum. Yet Korea was an especially savage war, where
millions were slaughtered in a scorched-earth policy. If
anything, Korea set the stage for how the US would later
attack Vietnam.

While American planes were firebombing Korean

towns and villages in the north, augmented by hundreds of tons of napalm, debate about whether or not to use nuclear weapons raged between Truman, the Joint Chiefs of Staff, and Gen. Douglas MacArthur, who was especially keen to nuke the living hell out of Korea. MacArthur believed that dropping thirty or so nuclear bombs would create a radioactive cobalt belt "from the Sea of Japan to the Yellow Sea," thus preventing a land invasion from the north for some sixty to 120 years. "My plan was a cinch," the old general insisted.

Before MacArthur could implement his cinchy plan, he was relieved of command by Truman, ostensibly for insubordination, but mainly because the mad General could not be trusted to carry out the more serious nuclear option being discussed by his superiors. Truman did not rule out nuking Korea, saying that the US would weigh any military strategy deemed necessary for total victory. Much of this rhetoric was aimed at the Chinese and Soviet leaderships, warning them that any heavy interference in Korea, or direct attacks on major US targets, would be met with mushroom clouds. (This had little effect on the Chinese, who saw the war as their own, and actively fought against US troops.) In the end, nuclear weapons were not used, and really weren't necessary. Destruction of the Korean peninsula, North and South, was so vast, the death toll so high, that all nukes would have added was a radioactive exclamation point.

Korea's ceasefire era, still precariously in place, saw rebuilding and power consolidation in both states, the North coalescing in a family-run dictatorship, the South run for a time by a military junta, giving way to a corporate-dominated economic zone. Perhaps not Douglas MacArthur's dream state, protected by radioactive cobalt, but decidedly serviceable to the West, specifically the US, which can take profitable advantage of the South's low wage sweatshop labor, while using the North as means to frighten the domestic population, justifying more military spending to protect us from the Commie Korean Nuclear Threat, wherever or whatever that happens to be.

Over the years, I've spoken to many Koreans, all from the South, about their divided country and how they felt about reunification, assuming this was ever a possible reality. The South Korean military officers I met while in the Army said all the right things about US policy in their land, but weren't as gung-ho for another war with the North as were a few American officers I knew. They despised the Northern regime, yet considered it to be a part of them, in a weird family way—like a wayward brother or cousin experimenting with an unacceptable lifestyle. In time, I was told, the wayward Northern brothers would see the light, and rejoin the South to make Korea one of the strongest states in Asia.

Twenty-some years later, with Korea still divided and

hostilities on a steady but low simmer, I found myself working nights in a small boutique mall in Michigan. By the time I was sweeping and mopping the food court's floors, the only remaining shop owner was a Korean immigrant named Kim, whose family operated a very successful lunch counter offering both American delicacies like hamburgers and BLTs, and Korean dishes like *kimchi*. Most nights Kim would patiently clean his grill, change the frying oil, scrub the counter and wash his dishes, singing what sounded like Korean country and western songs as he toiled. He and I exchanged small talk here and there, but one night, the subject of the Kwangju massacre came up, and I asked Kim what he knew of it.

"I was there!" he said, patting his chest. "I saw the soldiers shoot the people. It was a bad time."

Kim was a student activist, opposed to the Southern military regime. He stopped cleaning and told me what it was like—the tear gas, the bullets, the running and screaming. He spoke of the desire for political freedom, and how the junta had lied to the world about their "democracy" while destroying any independent challenge to their rule.

"I thought the South was *the* free Korea," I replied.

"Not then," said Kim, shaking his head. "Better now, but not as free as they say."

When I asked Kim what he thought of the North, he looked as though he had a bad tooth, scrunching his face with disdain. He was a Christian, and the North was run by atheists. He could never live under such a system. Still, Kim held out hope for national reunification. Most Koreans did, he told me. When or how would this happen? I asked. Kim looked around, as if to make sure no one was eavesdropping, then whispered, "When the Americans leave."

I assured Kim that this would never occur, at least not in our lifetimes. And the crazy thing was, if any US president could withdraw troops from Korea and get away with it domestically, he or she would be a Republican. There was no chance that a Dem president would oversee a pull-out, especially since the American presence began under a Dem administration. Never go against the family, as Michael Corleone warned his younger brother Fredo in *The Godfather*.

Kim laughed, then went back to scrubbing and singing. "Don't go against the family," he muttered, chuckling to himself.

CAMELOT MULE AND
THE BIG TEXAS JACKASS

I saw the Kennedy mystique up close in my teens. My father's second wife, a Dallas native, was to have been part of the group of schoolgirls who greeted JFK and Jackie with roses at Love Field. But she had become sick and couldn't go, a twist of fate that went on to haunt her. She kept all the newspapers from that day in pristine condition, taking them out occasionally to stare at the photo of her classmates handing Jackie a bouquet. She'd speak mystically about Kennedy—how he was her generation's father, snatched away in his prime. When the subject of Robert Kennedy arose, she'd cry and talk of promise unfulfilled. I never really understood her emotion, but it was clearly powerful and hardly unique. I encountered similar expressions later in life when mixing with various liberal crowds. By then I was aware of JFK's grisly record, as I assumed they were; yet the facts never dampened their love and appreciation.

Lee Harvey Oswald, or the mafia, or the CIA, or the Klingons, cemented John F. Kennedy's celestial status for eternity. Had the stylish president lived to see a second term, his glamorous visage would doubtless have crumbled, especially if the 1960s had played out as it did after his death.

"HEY, HEY JFK! HOW MANY KIDS DID YOU KILL TODAY?"

The chant is interchangeable, the rhythm undisturbed.

But wait, counter Kennedy-heads: had he lived, JFK would have pulled out of Vietnam, sparing the nation years of social unrest and division, while implementing and expanding a war-free New Frontier.

It's a pleasant narrative, something that soothes the nerves of many older liberals. But it's fiction, based on internal documents and the simple fact that no one really knows how JFK would ultimately have dealt with Vietnam. As late as September 1963, some six weeks before his death, Kennedy told CBS News icon Walter Cronkite, "I don't agree with those who say we should withdraw. That would be a great mistake." Whatever the reality, it was clear early on that the Camelot Mule was committed to massacring the Vietnamese, escalating direct US military involvement in November 1961, conducting hundreds of air assaults in the South, dropping napalm generously across the countryside.

While there were internal discussions about a possible

decrease in direct US involvement, the opposite actually occurred. By the time of JFK's assassination, plans were already drawn up for an expansion of American troops and combat missions due to the resilience of the Vietnamese resistance and the unstable Saigon regime of Ngo Dinh Diem, who was killed in a coup just before Kennedy got smoked. November 1963 was a season of political murder, from heads of state down to the Vietnamese peasants who failed to embrace American "assistance." Though there was talk that some troop reductions might coincide with military success, there was no serious indication that JFK sought a US with-drawal from the region.

Then came Dallas. The nation mourned as Lyndon Johnson took the oath, Vietnam falling into his crosshairs.

American political life has always been a feeding frenzy of delusion, uplift, and fantasy. Things that ought to be, are, and become so depending on the number of people agreeing to a particular concept and the need for that concept to be True. The myth of the peace-loving JFK remains one of the more durable fantasies, reinforced by Oliver Stone's film and by liberal apologists seeking to excise the holy Kennedy name from the Vietnam debacle. As Gore Vidal—who personally knew and liked Kennedy—has written, JFK loved war, and spoke about it in glowing terms. The man was prepared to blow up the planet in 1962 to remind the Soviets that only the

US may aim missiles near its enemy's border, not the other way around. While nuclear war over Cuba never happened, plenty of terror against Cuba itself—bombings, poisoning of crops, among myriad other delights—did indeed occur during Kennedy's presidency. His Alliance For Progress was a cover for death squad activity throughout the Americas, in an effort to rid the region of burgeoning Castros. And of course there was his murderous policy in Vietnam which, by the time of his death, had already destroyed swaths of the rural South.

JFK was a war criminal of the first order. Had he lived, he might have been one of the biggest in US history. Little wonder that his groupies still try to rinse the blood from his memory. Get assassinated and all is forgiven, or at least forgotten.

Lyndon Johnson didn't inspire the same emotions—not sympathetic emotions, anyway. LBJ was a veteran ballbuster, the kind of guy who'd slam your head against the wall until you saw things his way. Where Kennedy was chic, Johnson was crude, conducting staff meetings while taking a shit and draining bottles of Fresca. Still, you gotta hand it to LBJ: he simply didn't give a fuck. Egotistical, monomaniacal, large in frame and in ambition, Johnson stomped his way through Washington, bending wills and bashing brains. So it was no stretch for him to extend this rough approach to Vietnam, where the results were far worse than Beltway battles and wounded political pride.

It's interesting how a Texas populist, who wrote off the reactionary white South by signing the Civil Rights Bill, became one of the leading killers in Southeast Asia. LBJ may not have foreseen this down his professional road, but when given the opportunity he went after it in his usual manner: violently, without compromise or compassion. That the Vietnamese don't view Johnson as Americans view Osama bin Laden is a testament to their humanity. The blood-caked jackass made Charles Manson, Jeffrey Dahmer, and John Wayne Gacy look in comparison like the provincial amateurs they were.

There were two Democrats who early on opposed Johnson's escalation of war: Wayne Morse and Ernest Gruening, the only senators to vote against the Gulf of Tonkin Resolution in 1964. Yet despite the pair's avant-garde view of Vietnam, the majority of mules lined up behind their president, braying in unison for the need to slaughter those Vietnamese who had the audacity to shoot at American planes, boats, and soldiers—in their own country, no less!

From this point on, LBJ really let Vietnam have it, ripping up large portions of the country, routinely killing civilians not already caged in prison camps ("strategic hamlets"—a term with a nice Shakespearean ring), employing chemical warfare, free-fire zones, and kindred forms of persuasion. While opposition to Johnson's war crimes began to grow beyond the traditional pacifist and social justice movements, there was either assent or silence from most mainstream liberals. This would change somewhat by 1968, when LBJ was poised to run for re-election. By then, many elite figures and institutions had turned sour on the Vietnam enterprise, viewing it as a money-losing boondoggle that was unnecessarily creating too much domestic turmoil. This gave liberals the cover they needed to clear their throats and suggest that perhaps Vietnam was a "mistake," born only of the highest intentions. Walter Cronkite said so. Sometimes good ideas go bad. All one can do is try.

When the 1968 election season arrived, LBJ was a tired, spent man. A strong showing by antiwar candidate Eugene McCarthy in the New Hampshire primary, coupled with Robert Kennedy's entrance into the race, told the old mass murderer that his political career was kaput. Johnson threw in the towel in late March, allowing his vice president, Hubert Humphrey, a chance to succeed him as the nominee—which, with a boost from the Democratic Party machine, Humphrey did. Of course, Kennedy's assassination after winning the California primary helped Humphrey immensely, though he had enough delegates from non-primary states to fight off any Kennedy challenge at the Chicago convention. There's no indication that Sirhan Sirhan supported Humphrey—a rather doubtful idea, since Sirhan was Palestinian and Humphrey was solidly pro-Israel (as was Kennedy)—but he might as well have, given the end result.

While some liberals hoped that Humphrey, if elected, would end the war, the happy warrior didn't give that impression as he moved on to Chicago. Though he was heckled by antiwar students along the campaign trial, Humphrey appealed to old-line Dems as a bulwark against young radicals. His forces marginalized antiwar delegates at the convention, buoyed by Chicago Mayor Richard Daley's riot cops on the streets and plainclothes goons in the hall. As American firepower continued to slaughter Vietnamese, Humphrey smiled and waved from the convention podium, ignoring the fading chants of those opposed to the killing.

Many years after the 1968 election, Allen Ginsberg blamed young anti-war activists for Humphrey's narrow loss to Richard Nixon, saying that the kids had Vietnamese blood on their hands as Nixon, once in the White House, expanded US aggression. The implication, of course, is that President Humphrey would have ended the war much earlier, while maintaining the Great Society programs that LBJ had enacted, and that Nixon opposed.

We'll never know.

Still, absorbing the tenor of that time, it's difficult to take Ginsberg and others like him seriously. Wall Street may have given up "winning" the war, but state actors like Humphrey wouldn't—couldn't—concede defeat so easily. Though better domestically than Nixon—one true plaudit you can hand the guy—Humphrey gave no serious

ANTIWAR MULE CAMEO

As the Nixon era commenced, larger sections of the public turned against the war, with increasing numbers of Democrats joining them. While the language remained polite in most political mouths, Senator George McGovern of South Dakota provided spicier rebukes to the war-makers. At the Chicago convention, disaffected McCarthy and RFK supporters turned to McGovern as their antiwar symbol, none more passionate than Abe Ribicoff, a senator from Connecticut, who blasted Richard Daley's mini-police state by saying on national television, "And if George McGovern were president, we wouldn't have these Gestapo tactics in the streets of Chicago!"

McGovern wasn't president, but he stood in stark relief not only to Nixon, but also to pro-war figures in his Party like Henry "Scoop" Jackson, the "Senator from

Boeing" (and often-cited godfather to the neocons). On September 1, 1970, McGovern, along with antiwar Republican Senator Mark Hatfield, sponsored an amendment that called for the immediate withdrawal of US troops from Vietnam. Before the vote was taken, McGovern stood before the Senate and said:

> Every senator in this chamber is partly responsible for sending 50,000 young Americans to an early grave. This chamber reeks of blood. Every Senator here is partly responsible for that human wreckage at Walter Reed and Bethesda Naval and all across our land—young men without legs, or arms, or genitals, or faces or hopes.
>
> There are not very many of these blasted and broken boys who think this war is a glorious adventure. Do not talk to them about bugging out, or national honor or courage. It does not take any courage at all for a congressman, or a senator, or a president to wrap himself in the flag and say we are staying in Vietnam, because it is not our blood that is being shed. But we are responsible for those young men and their lives and their hopes.
>
> And if we do not end this damnable war those young men will some day curse us for our pitiful willingness to let the Executive carry the burden that the Constitution places on us.

So before we vote, let us ponder the admonition of Edmund Burke, the great parliamentarian of an earlier day: "A contentious man would be cautious how he dealt in blood."

McGovern's colleagues fell silent, and were so moved that they defeated the amendment by fifty-five votes to thirty-nine. The war continued, courtesy of a mule-controlled Senate.

Abe Ribicoff's wish for a McGovern presidency moved a bit closer to reality in 1972, as McGovern upset Party fixtures Edmund Muskie and Hubert Humphrey to grab the Dem nomination. But a seemingly chaotic convention, followed with VP choice Thomas Eagleton's admission that he had suffered depression and received electroshock treatments, sank McGovern's campaign before it took off. His attempt to unseat Nixon was probably quixotic at best, given that many mules were wary of McGovern. And the lack of presidential debates, in which McGovern would doubtless have gained strength, didn't help either. Still, in the face of these and other obstacles, McGovern ran an inspired campaign, and was the last Democratic nominee to take such an open antiwar stance. One of his commercials, where a Vietnamese mother carries her dead child down a deserted road, remains one of the strongest political ads in American history. Try to imagine a contemporary mule nominee doing the same with Iraq.

Nixon—the one killing Vietnamese children—was unaffected by such imagery, trouncing McGovern in the general election, and making Barry Goldwater's 1964 defeat by LBJ seem like a nail-biter.

With McGovern's loss, the antiwar Dems were cast adrift both in their Party and in the national culture— the term "McGovernite" coming to be considered the kiss of political death, most especially among liberals. Nixon's downfall in 1974 did little to alter this, despite opening a brief window for Idaho Senator Frank Church to conduct committee hearings on illegal FBI and CIA activity in 1975.

The Church Committee exposed numerous instances of government spying on American citizens, domestic political disruption, and US infiltration and subversion of foreign governments, as well as assassinations of foreign figures deemed hostile to US interests. While the Church Committee set in motion various oversight mechanisms, like the Foreign Intelligence Surveillance Act (FISA), its exposure of imperial criminality led to an inevitable back-lash—first with Jimmy Carter's faux "human rights" administration, and finally with Ronald Reagan's 1980 presidential win. The Gipper's coat-tails brought electoral victories to a number of right-wing Republicans that year, two of whom ousted Frank Church and George

McGovern, as clear a sign as any that the antiwar mule era was finished. The Democrats never again dared to reach so far.

MULE TEAM TAMED

To appreciate the antiwar Democratic collapse fully, you need look no further than the 1980s, when even the Liberal Media bowed before the majesty of Reagan's vaunted "revolution." There were some token holdouts. Speaker of the House Tip O'Neil made a big show about opposing Reagan's regressive policies, but in the end proved to be the backroom dealmaker that was his brand. Ted Kennedy also defended the old liberal guard, but he was more fixture than insurgent, his Camelot phrasing a nostalgic echo of a beloved but dead time. For the most part, the Dems were dazed and confused by Reagan's media-enhanced popularity, and scrambled to find their place in the new conservative epoch.

This is not to say that all Reagan-era Democrats rolled over or sought safe refuge. One of the more consistent Congressional critics of Reagan's policies, and of those senior Dems who enabled him, was Ron Dellums of California. Not only did Dellums oppose the renewed arms race started by Carter and carried on by Reagan, but he openly showed solidarity with official US enemies like Fidel Castro and Maurice Bishop of Grenada (the latter of whom was killed in an intra-party power grab that handed Reagan the pretext needed to invade the island). Dellums was naturally pilloried by domestic reactionaries as a traitor and Soviet stooge, while kept at arms length by the Democratic hierarchy. Yet Dellums remained popular enough with his constituents, and was returned to Congress until 1998, when he retired to become a (much criticized) lobbyist, then Mayor of Oakland.

But perhaps the sharpest anti-Reagan voice came from outside the Beltway machine. The Reverend Jesse Jackson, a former aide to Martin Luther King, Jr, repeatedly attacked the Reagan administration for its "constructive engagement" with apartheid South Africa, its massive military spending, and its terror wars throughout Central America. Jackson was also critical of US ties to Israel, highlighting human rights abuses against the Palestinians, and—even more outré—referring to them as human beings. This stance was taken by very few Democrats, certainly none coveting higher office. Yet such restrictions didn't apply to Jackson, who sought the Dem nomination in 1984 and 1988.

Jackson's first run had a real by-the-seat-of-your-pants

vibe, his Rainbow Coalition providing temporary shelter for various American progressives alienated from mainstream Democrats and repulsed by Reagan Republicans. But the RC proved to be a flimsy structure at best. I knew several people who worked on Jackson's campaign that year, which, at the grassroots, was all over the place. Jackson drew most of his strength from the anti-apartheid and Central American solidarity movements, and their concerns were amplified in Jackson's speeches and interviews—a serious jolt to the senses given the mood of that time. Leading Democratic candidate Gary Hart and eventual nominee Walter Mondale would never utter such radical statements—indeed, Mondale suggested a possible quarantine of Nicaragua, already under assault from the US. Jackson stood in direct opposition to this, and in the process won five primaries and caucuses. It was a bracing, if fleeting, moment.

Jackson's positions drew predictable derision from political elites; but the reverend went further, and fed his political opponents by referring to New York City as "Hymietown" in a discussion with the *Washington Post*'s Milton Coleman. While he did not pose a serious threat to seize the Democratic nomination, Jackson completely ruined whatever effect he might have had on the Party at that time. It was a stupid, racist blunder, for which Jackson repeatedly apologized, and which his tormentors continually decried. Of course, Jackson used only words.

Others, like Ronald Reagan, were actually murdering people of darker hue, whether through support of South African–backed terror proxies in that region's frontline states, or through the direct arming, training, and guidance of terrorist forces in Central America. No one of any prominence demanded apologies from Reagan or his henchmen. In fact, those who might have—say, the Democrats on Capitol Hill—were too busy looking for ways to help Reagan get around the minor restrictions placed on his aggression.

The most celebrated of these was the Boland Amendment, sponsored by Massachusetts Rep Edward Boland, which supposedly stemmed the flow of arms to the Nicaraguan Contras between 1982 and 1984, but in fact forced the Reagan gang to seek different avenues, which they easily found. When a bill supporting "humanitarian aid" to the Contras arrived in Congress in early 1986, leading progressives like Senator John Kerry voted for it, making a few "critical" noises in the process. The question of whether or not the US had the right to attack a smaller country that posed no physical threat was never asked, simply because the answer was internalized by those who could have made a difference. Thus continued the sorry, bloody spectacle of Democrats splitting the difference between "humanitarian" and "lethal" aid, while tens of thousands of Nicaraguans were butchered, tortured, maimed, and starved.

Still, as bad as that was, it paled in comparison to the Democratic capitulation to Reagan's terrorism when the weapons-for-hostages scandal known as Iran–Contra was exposed in late 1986. At first few took it seriously, since the initial news came from a Lebanese news outlet. But when the contours of the clandestine operation took definite shape, leading liberal columnists like Mark Shields and Richard Cohen of the *Washington Post* fell over each other trying to justify and excuse Reagan's involvement. John Chancellor of NBC News declared that the country could not afford another disgraced American presidency in the same generation as Watergate, and many political elites—regardless of party affiliation—agreed. From that point on, cover-up, dismissal, suppression and destruction of evidence, and round-the-clock rationalizing helped to squelch what, in a functioning constitutional democracy, would have been grounds for presidential impeachment and criminal prosecution. Instead, the US political system did what it does when a problem needs to be flushed: it held hearings.

The Iran–Contra hearings were both a national disgrace and an open look at how a powerful system adjusts to negative conditions. Chaired by Daniel Inouye, Democratic senator from Hawaii, the Iran–Contra Committee kept its focus as narrow as possible, protecting the identities of CIA operatives, ignoring the propaganda campaigns forged in the State Department and

National Security Council, wanting nothing to do with evidence of Contra drug running, and generally trying to keep the hearings from disrupting or disgracing business as usual. In one scripted scene, Inouye lambasted the existence of a "shadow government," saying how it was incompatible with a healthy democracy; but when Rep Jack Brooks of Texas attempted to question Oliver North about his plan to suspend the Constitution should a national crisis arise, Inouye cut Brooks off and ordered him to stop asking about "classified" matters. In this and other instances, "actual" and "shadow" governments over-lapped, with a senior Democrat overseeing and approving the process.

I watched most of these hearings in the office of FAIR—the media watch group for which I then worked—stunned by the slow-motion cover-up occurring before my eyes. I confess I was still politically green; not in thrall to the Democrats, yet not completely disgusted by American political reality. The Iran–Contra hearings, the overturned indictments, and subsequent presidential pardons of those involved with this phase of state terror served as a shovel to the head, knocking free whatever romantic notions I continued to harbor.

It was then that I swore never again to vote for a Democrat, no matter what the situation. Even when close friends worked for Jesse Jackson's 1988 campaign, when he won seven primaries and four caucuses, and was much more polished and effective than in 1984, I refused to participate, telling them that the Party would never nominate someone like Jackson. And it didn't, going instead with Michael Dukakis, who tried looking tough riding a tank, and, like Mondale before him, threatened Nicaragua—by then a bleeding, dying wreck, thanks to bipartisan efforts in the Beltway.

BUBBA MULE'S TWISTED HAYRIDE

Once Dukakis had been dispatched by Reagan's Veep George H. W. Bush, in a sleazy campaign that befuddled the dull mule team, liberals looked for a dazzling figure of their own, someone who could rebrand the Dem image. Many thought that the answer lay with New York Governor Mario Cuomo—an eloquent, forceful speaker who didn't shy from political battle (if there was something in it for him, that is) and it was believed that only Cuomo could defeat Bush in 1992.

But when Saddam Hussein invaded Kuwait in August 1990, Bush's military build-up in Saudi Arabia and subsequent bombing of Iraq in early 1991 made a Democratic victory the following year appear impossible. Bush's favorable poll numbers went over 90 percent as Americans threw victory parades, pounded their chests, and screamed to the skies, ecstatic that the Vietnam "syndrome" was finally dead. "USA! USA!" became the national chant, and not even the formidable Mario Cuomo wanted to fuck with that.

Still, nationalist frenzy carries one only so far, especially if there is little money in your pocket. Bush's war numbers began to slide along with the US economy, creating an opening for a Dem who, if savvy enough, could squeak past Bush on mainly economic grounds.

The savior liberals sought came from an unexpected place: Arkansas. At the 1988 Democratic convention, he had delivered what was considered the most boring speech in Party history. By 1992, he was anything but sleep-inducing.

Bill Clinton artfully blended Nixon's deviousness, Reagan's hokum, and JFK's sex appeal to become, and remain, a modern liberal darling. The spell he cast over Democrats cannot be overstated, it can only be admired—from a sick aesthetic angle, that is. I've spoken to self-described feminists who swooned like schoolgirls at the mention of his name. I've seen supposedly progressive men try to tap into his swagger and make it their own. No matter how awful his behavior or reactionary his stance, American liberals cannot get enough of the rube from Hot Springs.

Does their adoration come from hero worship? Appreciation of power? A desperate need to regain some kind of liberal hegemony, regardless of the actual cost?

Hard to say. Perhaps all these and more. Clinton arrived at a crucial moment for the mules, as twelve years of Reagan/Bush were sputtering to a close, and the only other serious contender for the Dem nomination was Jerry Brown. The former California governor had long been a political joke, but Brown displayed serious tenacity in his campaign, surging past the far more mainstream Paul Tsongas to challenge Clinton aggressively on various issues—the corrupt nature of the American political process being one of his main themes.

Naturally Brown was reviled by many observers, and after his strong showings in the Michigan and Illinois primaries, followed soon after by victory in the Connecticut primary, those behind Clinton were feeling the heat, as was Clinton's inner circle. As the New York and Wisconsin primaries approached, the media braced for the ultimate Dem showdown.

Two events occurred to swing the campaign Clinton's way. First, a story appeared on ABC News suggesting that drug parties were taking place at Brown's California residence while he was running for office. This rumor, widely believed to have originated with Clinton's "opposition research" team, came and went quickly; but it did put Brown, who angrily denied it, on the defensive. The second and perhaps most devastating blow to Brown was his announcement that he'd consider Jesse Jackson as a potential running mate. This didn't seem to hurt him in

Wisconsin, where he narrowly lost to Clinton. But it killed him in New York, and his campaign began fading from there.

At the time, Brown's run seemed somewhat miraculous, given the rancid political culture and the crooks who ran it in a very narrow direction. But in retrospect, Brown had no chance; had he won either Wisconsin or New York, or both, the Dem party elites would have done everything they could to sink him, as they were firmly behind Clinton, who could and did play as dirty as any candidate before or since. Besides, most liberals I knew hated Brown and feared that if he were the Party's nominee, Bush would have been re-elected easily. They liked Clinton precisely because he'd slit anyone's throat to win. And when he did win (helped mightily by Ross Perot's 19 percent of the popular vote), these liberals fell deeply in love with the new president.

Clinton was aware of this, and exploited it ably. While he made all the right sounds to placate the liberal wing, Clinton assured corporate power centers that he was a reliable servant and had their bottom lines at heart.

Clinton established a template for future mules to adopt and adapt, depending on political urgency. Although Clinton had worked on George McGovern's 1972 campaign, as president he was light years removed from such associations. He used enough of the few positive Democratic traits to color his rhetoric; but he also knew that his role was that of imperial manager, and that in the public mind no mule since JFK had so seamlessly blended high purpose with realpolitik, social grace with murderous intent. LBJ, Jimmy Carter, Walter Mondale, and Michael Dukakis couldn't achieve this critical balance. Bill Clinton could, and more or less did.

As a killer and status quo–enforcer, Clinton truly shone. An early example of this talent was seen in the government's surveillance of the Branch Davidian compound just outside Waco, Texas. The Bureau of Alcohol, Tobacco and Firearms (ATF), a paramilitary unit used for domestic control, became concerned with the large number of weapons and ammunition stockpiled in the compound. Branch Davidian leader and would-be messiah David Koresh was their chief target—allegations of child abuse and statutory rape making his demonization much easier to effect. When the ATF attempted an armed raid of the compound on February 28, 1993, the Davidians were waiting. A gunfight ensued, leaving four ATF agents dead, along with six Davidians. The ATF retreated, beginning a fifty-one-day standoff as the FBI assumed command of the tense situation.

During this standoff, Janet Reno was sworn in as Clinton's attorney general and conferred with the FBI about possible actions. It was clear that, after the killing of four federal agents, and with sixteen more wounded, the government wasn't going to wait forever to enforce its decree. Reno finally approved an FBI-planned siege, receiving the green light from Clinton. On April 19, the assault occurred, killing seventy-six Davidians, twenty-one of them children—seventeen of those under the age of twelve. The compound itself collapsed in flames, the government accusing the Davidians of setting the fire, critics of the operation saying that the feds had ignited the flammable CS gas that had filled the building. At least twenty Davidians were killed by gunfire. Senator John Danforth's investigative committee later insisted that these deaths were self-inflicted, while surviving Davidians claim they were under fire from FBI snipers.

The Waco siege showed that the Clinton administration could get medieval when necessary. To this day, Clinton defends what was done to the Davidians, with many liberals nodding in agreement. Janet Reno admitted that Waco was perhaps her darkest day as attorney general, and that in hindsight it could have been handled without the numerous charred bodies. While she stands by her decision to assault the compound, there is no confirmation that Reno suffers from a recurring nightmare in which the dead Davidian children float outside her bedroom window, scratching at the pane, inviting her to join them in play.

Waco not only inspired those liberals happy to see a Democrat kick ass; it also motivated a network of anti-statist activists—some bizarro right-wing, some simply libertarian, all in agreement that the federal government was too powerful, too violent, too ready to snuff out Constitutional protections. This opposition to Clinton took various forms, mostly peaceful and within the law, however hostile. But there was a surge in armed militias and talk of insurrection, and from this environment emerged Timothy McVeigh, the main actor behind the Oklahoma City bombing.

Depicted by the corporate press as the work of a deranged mind divorced from reality, the bombing of the Murrah Federal Building was explicitly intended as payback for Waco, the explosion occurring precisely two years to the day after Reno's assault. McVeigh killed 168 people, nineteen of whom were children. It was as cold-blooded and brutal as what happened to the Branch Davidians—the key difference being that Waco was state violence, and therefore defensible, whereas Oklahoma City was individual terrorism of the kind that sickens decent people. McVeigh tried to bridge these distinctions by writing in prison:

Do people think that government workers in Iraq are any less human than those in Oklahoma City? Do they think that Iraqis don't have families who will grieve and mourn the loss of their loved ones? Do people believe that the killing of foreigners is some-how different than the killing of Americans?

The double standard is obvious to those willing to see it. But coming from someone with innocent blood on his hands, the point gets lost amid the rubble and screams. McVeigh was executed in June 2001 to the applause of Clinton liberals—perhaps muted somewhat by the fact that McVeigh bought it under George W. Bush, and not their political hero. No Ricky Ray Rector rush for them.

Oklahoma City handed Clinton, and the American state, even more power, through the Antiterrorism and Effective Death Penalty Act of 1996. This was a real improvement on earlier police state models. It expanded presidential powers; pumped millions into SWAT and Delta teams, as well as the ATF; accelerated prison building; weakened habeas corpus for state prisoners; allowed for roving wiretaps; further restricted financial privacy; and made deportation of resident foreign aliens much easier, with no judicial review. More than anything else, the AEDPA set the table for the Patriot Act of 2001, and the subsequent abuses of FISA. In those later cases, liberals howled about attacks on the Constitution and the unique dangers of the Bush administration. Apart from assorted civil libertarian types, there had been no such liberal uproar when Clinton did the exact same thing.

When Clinton was re-elected in 1996, it appeared to the credulous that the Dems were truly back after twelve years of Republican White House rule. Unlike Jimmy Carter, Clinton got a second term; but then, unlike

Jimmy Carter, Clinton faced a weak Bob Dole rather than a robust Ronald Reagan. And besides, as in 1992, it was Clinton who wore Reagan's pompadour, with Dole playing the combined role of Carter and Walter Mondale. The GOP had no shot that year, and they knew it, which is why they offered up Dole for ritual sacrifice. They were looking ahead to 2000, when the presidential field would be wide open—or at least open enough to push an under-educated political scion on a public they despised and feared.

While further marginalizing and constraining the domestic population—primarily those with little to no economic or political power—Clinton remained busy internationally, selling arms to states at war with their own populations; or, in Israel's case, at war with stateless people trapped in a rotting cage. He sent record amounts of military aid to the Colombian government, which promptly and ruthlessly made good use of it, keeping the death squads fluid and well-stocked for business. Clinton also bombed Iraq on a regular basis, launching Tomahawk missiles into civilian neighborhoods, creating "collateral damage" as a reminder to Saddam Hussein that he should never have crossed his American superiors who, when inconvenienced, become quite unforgiving. In addition to aerial assaults, Clinton kept the murderous sanctions on Iraq, killing anywhere from half a million to a million Iraqis (numbers like these are sketchy since, as we've seen more recently, Iraqi lives really don't count). When his secretary of state, Madeline Albright, famously told Lesley Stahl on *60 Minutes*, "I think this is a very hard choice, but the price—we think the price is worth it," it became sparkling clear that the Clinton gang murdered with eyes wide open. They knew exactly what they were doing, and felt no need to apologize.

Although in scale and utter human misery, Clinton's strangling and pounding of Iraq was his supreme imperial achievement, his followers prefer to cite his bombing of Yugoslavia as Clinton's masterpiece, a "humanitarian" work of art that continues to make liberals ooh and aah in appreciation.

Painted as defense against Serbian fascism, Clinton's build-up to his seventy-eight-day bombing spree in the Spring of 1999 had more to do with expanding Nato's power base in Europe, sweetening the financial and geopolitical position of the US and its partners. Slobodan Milosevic, a Serbian nationalist surrounded by unsavory characters, was right out of central casting. That he was brutal to those who opposed him or wished to secede from the motherland definitely assisted Clinton's gang as they made their "humanitarian" case for military intervention. Liberal columnists like Anthony Lewis and William Pfaff cranked up anti-Serb sirens on Clinton's behalf, telling their educated readers why it was imperative that American cruise missiles teach this Nazi race a few things about responsible global behavior. After all, as Madeline Albright once put it while wiping Iraqi blood from her shoes, "If we have to use force, it is because we are America. We are the indispensable nation. We stand tall. We see further into the future."

The primary justification for Nato's bombing was that Serbian security forces had committed "genocide" in Kosovo, and that Milosevic not only knew about this but celebrated it—doubtless while sitting in a large leather chair, stroking a white cat, laughing maniacally as his fiendish plan took savage shape. Again, the reality was a bit murkier than the Ian Fleming scenario advanced by Clinton's gang and their liberal mouthpieces in the press. Serbian forces were indeed quite violent in Kosovo, as was the Kosovo Liberation Army, a paramilitary group not known for its gentle demeanor and embracing of democratic norms. The generally accepted number of Kosovar Albanian dead in the pre-Nato bombing period is around 2,500. Nasty. Horrible. But "genocide"?

If what the Serbs did in Kosovo was genocidal, then how to define what Clinton did in Iraq? Or what JFK/LBJ/Nixon did in Vietnam? Or what Reagan did in Central America? When confronted with these and similar comparisons, liberal imperialist writers like Samantha Power simply reject the term as applied to the US—for fairly obvious, professional reasons. One's public career does not advance when taking a wider view of slaughter.

Even more transparent, yet not perceived by swivel-chair commandos, was that some of the worst ethnic cleansing of that period took place within Nato itself: Turkey's ongoing war against the Kurds. As Western liberals cried and shook their fists at Milosevic, the Turkish state murdered around 30,000 Kurds, destroyed over 3,000 villages, and created 2–3 million refugees. And who sold the Turkish military the weapons and fighter jets used for this bloody campaign? Bill Clinton, the heroic figure fighting fascism in the Balkans.

When Milosevic refused to accept the conditions laid out in the Rambouillet accords, according to which US and Nato forces would enjoy "unimpeded access" throughout Yugoslavia, would take control of Serbian telecommunications "needed for the Operation, as determined by Nato," among many other privileges, the Serbian leader was pilloried by the Clinton gang as rejecting peace, and thus had to learn the hard way. From March 24 to June 10, Clinton's air assault raged, killing over 2,000 civilians with cluster bombs and depleted uranium munitions, targeting numerous civilian sites, as well as petrochemical plants, causing further toxic poisoning of the country. In Kosovo, Serbian forces reacted violently against the Albanian population, as had been predicted before the bombing began. And again, while brutal, it was not remotely "genocidal," if that word retains any serious meaning. The high body-count announced at the end of hostilities, when Nato occupied Kosovo and settled in for the long haul, dropped continually over the following months, as ever fewer bodies were discovered than had been predicted—and many of those that were could not be accurately depicted as victims of war crimes.

To the liberals who supported this "humane" aggression (which included Senator Paul Wellstone of Minnesota, who occasionally challenged Clinton, but not when it came to bombing Yugoslavia, and a year earlier, Iraq), it didn't matter. Nor did the mass ethnic cleansing of Serbs and Gypsies from Kosovo, accompanied by countless reprisal killings. What *did* matter was that a modern mule president gave them permission to embrace imperial violence and the double-standard that excuses it—for only the noblest reasons, naturally. So unlike Republican warmongers, who cheer mass murder because they're evil and stupid.

MULES TRUDGE RIGHTWARD, BRAY FOUL

After eight years of Clinton, American liberals were confident that Al Gore would easily extend the mini-dynasty for another term, if not two. Gore was part of a largely popular administration, faced only mild resistance from Bill Bradley in the primaries, and was set to combat George W. Bush—by all accounts a political lightweight with a mind to match, a second-rate version of his mediocre father.

I remember the confidence and arrogance from my professional liberal friends. Gore would smash little Bush to bits and win the presidency with ease. It would be a laugh-fest of a campaign: confirmation that Clintonite centrism and triangulation worked, and provided the winning model for all future Dem efforts. As Clinton had tapped Gore to strengthen his right flank, Gore chose Joe Lieberman, a very conservative mule who was also a

leading cultural scold. The 2000 Dem ticket was perhaps
the most rightist pairing in recent Party history—something that liberals celebrated and supported with few if
any serious reservations.

While Democrats assured themselves of continued
success, Ralph Nader began his presidential run as the
Green Party's nominee. Nader represented those shut out
of and fed up with the corporate Democratic structure,
his campaign an open rebuke to the mules' rightward
drift. Initially, Gore liberals paid little attention to Nader,
viewing his run as at best a pitiful joke. But as Campaign
2000 heated up, and Nader's poll numbers hovered
between 5 and 9 percent, depending on region, it became
clear to the Democrats that a growing slice of "their"
base rejected the national ticket. And since Dems insist
that all left-of-center voters owe their allegiance to the
Party, this insubordination was intolerable. That's when
the liberals declared war on Nader—a jihad that continues
to this day.

It wasn't a pretty sight. For all of their supposed
tolerance and open-mindedness, American liberals can be
and often are incredibly sectarian, especially where their
Party is concerned. They usually try to mask this by
claiming that they are pragmatists and realists, given the
way the two-party system is set up. Third parties stand
no chance, are exercises in political vanity—and, worse,
weaken the prospects of a flawed but in essence truly

progressive party. Of course, this very narrow reasoning inevitably leads back to voting for Democrats only. If you want to protest against the status quo, do so in the primaries, where you'll be given token representation before being shown the door by the managers of Serious Candidates, who don't have time for all that "principled" bullshit. Speaking the truth is for losers and egomaniacs.

I was drawn to Nader's campaign mainly on political grounds, since I agreed with much of his platform. But it was the enthusiasm of Nader's super-rallies that really pulled me in. The rally I attended was standing-room only, multi-racial, multi-generational, passionate, electric, inspiring. Over the years I had attended many Democratic rallies and gatherings, and they were stiff, choreographed affairs. Nader's gathering was much different. There were shared, spontaneous outbursts of democratic emotion, and the prevailing mood was one of grassroots citizenship. And of course Nader said things that Gore and Bush wouldn't have uttered even at gun-point: how bankrupt the present system is; how politics are privatized; how corporations and their political clients are raping whatever's left of constitutional protections; how US foreign policy is based on war and exploitation.

It made an aging, crusty cynic like myself feel alive. That's when I joined Nader's campaign.

When I told this to some of my professional liberal friends, they went ballistic. One woman, who worked for

Dem causes on Capitol Hill, informed me that supporting
Nader was a right-wing, racist act, and then never spoke
to me again. Others simply called me idiotic, utopian, clue-
less. Didn't I know that, despite his mainstream rhetoric,
Al Gore was the real progressive populist in the election?
Oh, sure, he supported Nafta, the death penalty, Israeli
aggression, and the regular bombing of Iraq—but hey, no
one's perfect, and for Gore to win, he had to adopt
some disagreeable positions. Nader's talk about systemic
corruption, while probably true, wouldn't appeal to the
mass population. And besides, the Greens were a bunch of
old hippies lost in time. Who cared what they thought?

For me, the main goal was to help Nader grab the 5
percent of the vote needed to award the Greens federal
matching funds, which would help to build a small,
potentially effective alternative party. Still, I wasn't crazy
about many of the Greens themselves. Some of the meetings I attended and individuals I met lacked much of
the spontaneity I experienced at the major rally. And
yes, there were smatterings of old hippies here and there.
But there were also numerous enthusiastic young people
who weren't Greens by name. The party's structure, as
far as I could tell, was decidedly shaky when not simply
chaotic. But this was the only political alternative that
attracted large groups of volunteers and activists. The
Greens would have to do, blemishes and all.

An old friend and colleague of mine worked directly

for Nader that year, and he kept me inside the loop, which helped somewhat. (He also got me to write two Top Ten lists for Nader's appearance on David Letterman.) As the campaign moved into the fall and continued to attract huge audiences nationwide, the long Dem knives really came out.

Nader was continually attacked by Gore/Lieberman partisans and personnel, aggressively painted as a Bush enabler and co-conspirator, despite the fact that the mule ticket had more in common with the GOP ticket than Nader had with either camp. No matter. The strategy was to turn Nader into some regressive political menace while keeping him away from major election venues like the presidential debates. The last thing either ruling party wanted was Nader sharing the stage with Gore and Bush— too dangerous for democracy.

The Commission on Presidential Debates, controlled by representatives of both parties, not only refused to invite Nader to state his case to millions of voters, but physically blocked him from entering any hall or auditorium where the debates took place. When Nader showed his ticket to Commission authorities in Boston, he was denied access and threatened with arrest, with no explanation given. Now, American politics has long been a corrupt and dirty game controlled by those with the power to enforce their will, so none of this is really a surprise. Still, given all the pious warnings about Ralph Nader's anti-democratic tendencies, it was the Democrats who employed any tactic, from open slander to physical force, to keep Nader marginalized and out of Al Gore's way.

Some in the Green camp called the Dems cowards afraid of an actual debate, which they were. But it made sense in gritty political terms, and it worked. Nader's poll numbers began to slip, and by election day the magic 5 percent had dwindled down to just over 2 percent. Gore liberals successfully kept their candidate away from serious inquiry, while scaring numerous potential Nader voters back into the Dem fold.

While the mules helped deny the Greens federal matching funds, thus eliminating any serious political challenge down the road, they lost ground against a very beatable Bush, their extreme focus on Nader perhaps sapping whatever anti-GOP strength they possessed.

When the deadlock occurred in Florida, it was the Republicans who showed crazed rigor and an animated desire to swing the supposedly tied vote their way. The Dems, taking their cue from the man they had worked so hard to insulate from Nader's critiques, appeared listless in response. Whatever ballot fraud or irregularity existed, liberals suddenly lacked the partisan venom they had expended on Nader. Instead of creating a loud, political din, clogging Florida streets with direct action, raising whatever ceaseless hell it took to get an accurate re-count of that state's vote, Gore supporters went along with their leader, who had no stomach for a bloody fight. Gore insisted on re-counts in only four counties, instead of the entire state, and his timidity cost him the election.

Nader's critique of Gore's allegiance to the status quo was borne out in Florida. Gore put the corrupt system ahead of political justice, for the "sake of the nation," then slunk away from the national limelight to lick the minor scratches received in his brief, pitiful fight. Left stranded by their candidate, liberals turned their ire on Nader, who they blame for pretty much every negative thing that has occurred since 2001, tsunamis and hurricanes included.

My inbox filled with nasty emails from those liberals still talking to me—everything from "Happy now?" to "You have blood on your hands," and similar invective in between. They had no interest in discussing what had actually happened—primarily Gore's cowardice and dreadful campaign, but also why they weren't as bent about David McReynolds and Monica Moorehead, two lefty independents whose combined 2,426 votes may also have cost Gore Florida, if their charges against Nader had any meaning. It was much simpler and personally more satisfying to blame Nader for "stealing" votes pre-owned by Gore. To them, independent political expression is far worse than the rigid, tainted system itself. And there's a good reason for that: liberals like the system as it is. They just want to run it.

MULES AGAINST TERROR

Less than a year after their leader's capitulation, American liberals were faced with the fresh horror of being tarred as soft on Islamofascism.

The 9/11 terror attacks could be spun only one way, regardless of who occupied the White House: rightward. Indeed, had Gore been president when the planes hit, he doubtless would have been slammed as asleep at the wheel by the domestic phalange. Whether or not the larger population would share this reaction is another question, as Americans tend to give their presidents unqualified support during a national crisis. As it happened, Bush received a blank check to do pretty much whatever he and his cronies desired, and this put Democrats and liberals on the defensive. (Many liberals, primarily bloggers, contend that President Gore would have prevented the 9/11 attacks, arresting Mohammad Atta and his gang well before that deadly day. Given how events played out, soothing reveries are to be expected.)

Amid the frenzied flag-waving and outbursts of raw nationalism that followed the attacks, Democrats went out of their way to flash their patriotic credentials, hands on hearts, anthems in throats, eyes misty red. Then came the martial rhetoric, perhaps best deployed by Sen. Hillary Clinton, poised to fill the gap left by Gore:

> We will also stand united behind our President as he and his advisors plan the necessary actions to demonstrate America's resolve and commitment. Not only to seek out an exact punishment on the perpetrators, but to make very clear that not only those who harbor terrorists, but those who in any way aid or comfort them whatsoever will now face the wrath of our country. And I hope that that message has gotten through to everywhere it needs to be heard. You are either with America in our time of need or you are not.

Either/or. Ever the fast learner, Hillary projected the Bush vibe early and effectively. This would come in handy down the dead-littered road.

Since al-Qaeda enjoyed the hospitality of the Taliban regime in Afghanistan, it was clear that American "daisy cutters" would soon add to that country's vast collection of rubble. When Bush gave the order to strike, his poll numbers soared. Not wanting to be left out of the action, the Democrats and most liberals cheered Bush on, because now we were all Israelis, or Brits during the blitz, or Bruce Willis in *Die Hard*, walking barefoot on broken glass, bringing the final hammer down on the terrorists, with a yippie ki yay, motherfucker.

Amazingly, there was one Congressional Democrat who opposed this extremely popular scenario: Barbara Lee of California. Her brief but impassioned speech on the House floor three days after the attacks stood out in a dense atmosphere of rage and calls for merciless reprisal, and it must be one of the more courageous public stands in Congressional history. Of course, Lee was immediately pilloried, her life threatened, her image flashed all over the Web as the face of domestic treason. She had to know this was coming, and yet she stood her ground regardless. Not many Democrats can say that.

At the time, I admired Lee's stance, but the assault on New York bent me in ways I still cannot fully fathom— apart from the base horror of seeing my beloved city seriously wounded, that is. The sight of liberals flying the flag afterward didn't move me to derision as it usually had. While I was not a born-again nationalist, neither was I contemptuous of this expression. I had no desire to become a Savage Mule, but the idea of war grew favorably in my twisted mind.

Much of this stemmed from my being an Army veteran. Though it was my exposure to military life that had politicized and then radicalized me, when I enlisted I was receptive to the propaganda, and marched through boot camp with a determined smile and a well-oiled weapon. The seed they plant in you during that period takes some kind of root; and no matter where you end up, that early feeling remains in some form. It may have taken a few months, but after the 9/11 attacks and the US invasion of Afghanistan, I was fully one with the killing machine. Barbara Lee's sensible, sane advice evaporated in my head, replaced with the glorious noise of cluster bombs ripping apart jihadists and their enablers.

To say that I was out of my mind back then would be an understatement. The bile, the hatred, the lust for violence and death drowned me. And I was placed, whether I liked it or not, squarely with the Savage Mules, among numerous, ranting others. But even here, I thought that the Dems were too cautious, not nearly crazy enough. I felt that, for all of their stated war support, liberals lacked the necessary, sadistic edge. It's a testament to my insanity that I took such concepts seriously.

While nearly every liberal I knew supported the Afghan war, seeing it as an act of self-defense, not all were enthusiastic with Bush's push to invade Iraq. Much of this had to do with the fact that they opposed Bush politically, and not that they were antiwar or anti-imperialist. Many supported

Clinton's bombing of Yugoslavia, and said or did practically nothing while Clinton bombed and choked off Iraq. Had Clinton been president after 9/11 and desired an invasion of Iraq (a natural extension of his policy of sanctions and bombing) as part of the War on Terror, chances are extremely high that a vast majority of liberals would have supported him, based on their previous allegiance.

Instead, the Thief Executive, the Chimp in Charge, was blowing the trumpet, and most liberals weren't buying it. When their president-in-exile Al Gore spoke out against Bush's plans (though Gore's "opposition" was merely tactical, saying that he supported building a coalition to take on "Saddam Hussein in a timely fashion"), this gave those mules added incentive to oppose the Iraq war. Still, there were many liberals and Dems who wanted to displace Saddam immediately, who believed Bush's claims about vast stockpiles of WMD, and—perhaps dizziest of all— expressed a desire to install Western-style democracy in at least one Arab country, showing the natives at gunpoint why we are the envy of the world.

When voting to authorize US aggression against Iraq in October 2002, eighty-one House Democrats sided with Bush, while twenty-nine of fifty Senate Democrats did the same. Among the big names backing the invasion were Diane Feinstein, Charles Schumer, John Kerry, Tom Daschle, Joe Biden, Chris Dodd, Harry Reid, Joe

Lieberman—and, of course, Hillary Clinton, whose experience in a war-making White House gave her added insight when it came to killing even more Iraqis.

I'm very sorry to say that I nearly joined this squalid chorus. Friend, former mentor, and leading lefty hawk Christopher Hitchens, who convinced me to back the Afghan invasion, worked hard to get me to see the added glory of an Iraqi campaign. While he hoped for a large Baathist body count, he insisted that the invasion would go smoothly, that there would be token resistance, that the now anti-imperial US military would occupy Baghdad and usher in a progressive, secular rebirth in the heart of that long-suffering region. It all sounded good—too good, in fact. But what if Hitch was right? What genuine progressive could dismiss the possible democratization of Iraq? Maybe things had really changed. Maybe this was a crucial historical turning point. Wouldn't I want to be on the right side of such an important moment in time?

While I was on the cusp of bellowing for another US invasion, a small but steady voice inside my head pleaded with me to stop. Like the proverbial splinter in the brain, this voice irritated me, nagged at me, insisted that I seriously rethink everything I had been advocating and was about to endorse. I thought back to the lead-up to the first Gulf War, went through all my old files—pieces of talks that I had given, articles I had clipped for

reference, transcripts of various debates. I felt as though
I was examining a dead man's earlier life, piecing together
his political outlook through notes and papers he considered useful and inspirational. Then I found an old *Harper's*
cover piece from January 1991, written by the same man
who was nudging me to share his pro-invasion position.
I sat and read it for the first time in ages, and then I
got to the end:

> The call [to war] was an exercise in peace through
> strength. But the cause was yet another move in the
> policy of keeping a region divided and embittered, and
> therefore accessible to the franchisers of weaponry and
> the owners of black gold. An earlier regional player,
> Benjamin Disraeli, once sarcastically remarked that you
> could tell a weak government by its eagerness to resort
> to strong measures. The Bush administration uses strong
> measures to ensure weak government abroad, and has
> enfeebled democratic government at home. The
> reasoned objection must be that this is a dangerous and
> dishonorable pursuit, in which the wealthy gamblers
> have become much too accustomed to paying their
> bad debts with the blood of others.

That small, irritating voice in my head suddenly became
clear. Back the Iraq invasion? What the fuck was I thinking?
This was merely the next phase of the same regional war,

conducted for the same, geopolitical reasons. Democracy?
Pluralism? Christ, we barely have that here, so why in
hell would we give the Iraqis something that we're curtail-
ing at home? And anyway, how do you "give" someone
democracy? This was lunatic rhetoric used to cover a
time-honored, blood-coated shell game. The old Hitchens
was absolutely right. The new Hitchens was a willing,
well-paid, imperial stooge. I knew which side I was on,
all right, and I decided to tell Hitch the bad news and
hopefully try to change his mind.

Well, clearly that never happened. Hitchens was at
first surprised, then testy, then angry, then haughty and
dismissive, before finally severing all ties. I had collaborated
with the enemy, which meant I was lost, and therefore
technically dead. Hitchens had another war to promote,
and doubtless a few more after that, and since I was on
the Other Side . . .

My waking up before the Iraq debacle led me to
reconsider my support for the Afghanistan campaign. After
the initial euphoria, at least here in the West, about how
wonderful things were in that battered country, and how
it could only get better, the reality of that war began to
emerge. A massive famine may have been averted in the
early days, but people were still starving, living under
conditions that we wouldn't allow our house pets to
endure, while their children were dying of dehydration
and disease at an astonishing rate. For all the hype about

schools being opened and kite-flying allowed, nothing had really changed.

Yes, the Taliban have been bombed out of power, but not out of the country, nor out of the lives of those Afghans who still support them, or are terrorized into giving them shelter. While the Taliban were backed and recognized by Pakistan, they remain part of Afghanistan, and didn't materialize out of thin air. We can bomb, and bomb, and bomb, but they'll never go away, which of course gives us further pretext to bomb and bomb for years on end. And our bombing gives the Taliban, and others like them, an immediate pretext to set off car bombs and IEDs for as long as they have access to explosives and weapons—which in Afghanistan, with all of its arms smuggling, will be a very long time. So cluster bomb casualties lead to car bomb fatalities, then back to more cluster bomb casualties, and on and on it will go—maybe a decade, maybe more—while the Afghan poor continue to die, and Kabul is run by kleptocrats, hustlers and mercenaries. Democracy was never on the agenda, and after years of pounding, the very word is an obscenity uttered over a fully functioning, open mass grave.

Unfortunately, my personal sojourn had nothing to do with what American elites had in mind, conservative and liberal alike. On March 20, 2003, the invasion and subsequent occupation of Iraq began, and will doubtless continue for the rest of our lives, in one form or another.

If not, you have my permission to burn this book—but only if you bought it first.

After cruising across the desert and quickly setting up shop in Baghdad and elsewhere, American and British forces noticed that a growing number of Iraqis resented their presence. What was celebrated as a swift victory quickly succumbed to an increasingly violent insurgency, aimed not only at occupation troops, but at foreign mercenaries, Western civilians—and, perhaps most ruthlessly, at Iraqis of different classes and religious affiliations. Before long, the country began ripping apart, turning an already miserable situation into an hourly hell on earth. It was a corpse-strewn nightmare, and the liberals and Dems who had supported it scrambled for explanations, placing blame everywhere except in their own mirrors.

One of the more popular complaints from pro-war liberals was that Secretary of Defense Donald Rumsfeld failed to "win the peace" by not clamping down on rioting Iraqis in the invasion's wake. Equally popular was the mantra that Rumsfeld sent too few troops to secure adequately what was rightly ours. These criticisms were regularly heard on Air America, the "progressive" answer to right-wing radio, whose biggest star, Al Franken, had supported the invasion. Before long, they were standard talking points for many liberal bloggers as well. When it became obvious that there were no WMD, that the prime rationale for the invasion had turned out to be a lie,

Democrats sensed that this would give them the opening needed to win back the White House in 2004—even if they had backed Bush's war from the jump, like John Kerry.

A Vietnam combat vet who was slightly to the left of Al Gore, Kerry cast a wider, if not the widest net, bringing in not only the Dem faithful but those who felt guilty about having supported Nader over Gore. There were also those, like me, who felt no guilt about exercising free political choice, but believed that another four years of Bush would be disastrous for the world, and we grudgingly supported Kerry's campaign—in my case, turning away from the anti-mule pledge I had made in 1988. Not that I was unaware of Kerry's shortcomings and his own imperial concepts; but it seemed that Bush was unprecedented in his criminality, and that replacing him with a lesser crook would help to slow the rancid tide until a broader opposition could be forged.

Pie in the exploding sky? No doubt. But other than abstaining, what choice was there? Nader ran again, only this time as farce, with no semblance of a broader political agenda. If one truly wanted to remove Bush, Kerry was the only option, no matter how awful he proved to be.

I took the 2004 election so seriously that I actually worked for the Kerry/Edwards campaign. I phone-banked, stuffed envelopes, drove people around, and spent time talking to Kerry operatives in the local office. Once again,

I was reminded why I despise the Democrats so. Most of these people were youngish white men seeking some kind of political career with the Party. All they cared about was winning elections. Talking actual politics, as opposed to Party-approved bullet-points, proved fruitless, as many of them had no idea what was going on in the wider world. Nor did they know much about the history of the Party they had chosen to serve. On top of this, some of these guys were incredibly snide and short-tempered with the volunteers, the majority of whom were senior citizens. They set themselves up as political wizards to be blindly obeyed, rather than co-workers looking to oust Bush. I spent less and less time in those offices, though I put in a full day on election day, trying to avoid any serious contact with these dicks, who were openly worried that Bush would win, and were coming apart at the seams.

Kerry came close, and there are those who say that Ohio was stolen from him through massive voter fraud and suppression. It wouldn't surprise me. Electoral cheating is a proud American tradition. Still, one shouldn't underestimate the spell that crude, nativist rhetoric casts over a significant number of Americans. Bush was popular to millions, as he tossed them plenty of carcasses to gnaw on. If his operatives helped things along by stealing votes, well, that's politics. Besides, it's doubtful that Kerry, the reluctant anti-warrior, would have ended the Iraq occupation. He certainly didn't advocate a speedy withdrawal. If anything, he might well have increased troop numbers in order to cap sectarian violence—a surge of his own, as it were. Yet, as with the fantasy Gore administration, we'll never know.

Kerry's loss put added pressure on Democrats to flash anti-terror credentials of their own, if only to gain ground in the 2006 midterm elections. They found a ripe issue in the Dubai Ports deal, when the Bush administration hired the United Arab Emirates company to secure six major American ports against nefarious bin Ladenist plots.

It was one of the more opportunistic, cynical and asinine displays in recent memory.

American liberals were dying to prove how they, unlike the GOP, were the "real" guardians of American lives and property. From Hillary Clinton, to Air America, to Daily Kos and numerous other libloggers, "Portgate" was all the rage, an opportunity to flex their fantasy muscles and jump on the Arab-bashing bandwagon. DNC Chairman Howard Dean, appearing before the Jewish Council for Public Affairs in early 2006, said, "Today we see the specter, as reported in the *Jerusalem Post*, of a company who is about to take over American ports, which actively continues today to boycott Israel."

The fact that Dubai Ports had worked with Israel seemed to escape Dean's attention, as well as the fact that the UAE was wholly loyal to US/Israeli regional policy, official propaganda aside.

Of course, this liberal yowling had nothing to do with "national security" and everything to do with taking full advantage of a political opening, using the very xenophobic weapons that are part of the reactionary arsenal. Not only did the Dubai Ports hysteria further prove that the War on Terror is a crock, it emphasized all too well that no real opposition to the corporate status quo exists—at least in the ownership parties. Instead of examining the business-as-usual aspect of the Dubai Ports deal, and how the American ruling elite and their political lackeys benefit from such global financial arrangements, liberals preferred to fan jingoist flames for domestic political gain. The Arab booga-booga worked both ways and for the same purpose: power.

But what was truly amusing in all the pretend uproar was the heroic posture of those who didn't want to deal with a state boasting "terrorist" ties. Whatever involvement the UAE had in aiding terrorism, it didn't remotely approach the violent level of Israel, Turkey, Colombia, or even—gasp!—the United States. Yet you'd never hear mainstream liberals making this much noise over arms sales to these and other countries. Indeed, when the Clinton administration sold the UAE eighty F-16 Block 60 fighters in 1998, there was no outrage from the liberal corner, or concern that their idol Bill Clinton was aiding and abetting "terrorism"—and this was at the very moment when the UAE had recognized the Taliban regime in

Afghanistan, one of the criminal indictments that liberals hurled at the oil nation while attacking the ports deal.

"Portgate" was yet another domestic political ruse that said nothing about the global corporate power structure that makes such deals inevitable, nor about what truly constitutes terrorism in the here and now. It was simple, sleazy fear-mongering—another reminder that the Democrats have the same contempt for the populace as do GOP reactionaries.

Later that same year, many Democrats also showed their contempt for the Lebanese and Palestinians when they openly supported Israel's shelling of Lebanon, and further aggression against the Gazans.

During a large pro-war rally at the United Nations, attended by many of New York's elected officials and those seeking office, Dan Gillerman, Israel's ambassador to the UN, asked, presumably of his patrons, "Let us finish the job" to "excise the cancer in Lebanon." Israeli officials have long referred to Arabs who might resist them, primarily Palestinians, as a cancer. (Similar language was used by German Nazi leaders and their followers to describe Jews.) Gillerman added that Hezbollah and Syria had "raped" Lebanon, which, coming from a representative of a country that was then shredding Lebanon to pieces, was somewhat rich. Not that Gillerman denied this reality. Responding to the timid, tactical criticism that Israel was unleashing "disproportionate" violence upon Lebanon, Gillerman replied, "You're damn right we are."

Among the American politicos present, it was Hillary Clinton who really had Gillerman's back: "We will stand with Israel because Israel is standing up for American values as well as Israeli ones." No doubt.

Much of American "progressive" radio followed suit, to the degree that hosts even discussed Israel's bombing campaign. Liberal chat host Ed Schultz was perhaps the most outspoken, bellowing into his mike on July 13, "I support Israel!" because "Israel is a democracy" and "the Palestinians are not innocent." He added that Hezbollah was to Israel what North Korea was to the US. Yes, Schultz actually made that comparison in an effort to get his listeners to appreciate Israel's fear. Of course, the IDF didn't then fear Hezbollah, seeing that they possessed superior firepower and were backed by the US; but Schultz tried to make it seem that Israel was being cornered by Hezbollah, just as we might be cornered by the mighty North Korean state in the near future.

A few days later, on July 17, Schultz was at it again, comparing Lebanon to Nazi Germany and the Israeli air force to American and British bombers valiantly striking its fascist infrastructure. Any serious historian would immediately embrace Schultz's analogy, especially when you consider how Lebanon's numerous panzer divisions rolled through the Middle East, reducing nations like

Israel to rubble, and herding the survivors into camps. As Schultz reminded his listeners, many of whom expressed even nastier views on the ongoing violence, we killed plenty of German civilians, too. Part of war. No getting around it.

Among liberal bloggers, there was mostly silence. Apart from getting mules elected and trading raspberries with Republicans, most online liberals aren't all that interested in how their tax dollars are spent overseas. I mean, are the Gazans even registered Democrats?

AMONG THE KOSSACKS

When Juan Cole, professor of history at the University of Michigan, invited me to join his panel at YearlyKos, I was flattered yet skeptical. Juan and I are friends, live in the same town, get together now and then for ales and political discussion. All fine and good. But speaking at a liberal convention to an audience of loyal Democrats and related hangers-on? Didn't seem like a winning notion to me. The very idea filled me with contempt.

I'm not part of the liblogger world; I don't play first-name footsie with the big liberal faves; I'm not looking to belong to or redeem the mule party. If Juan wasn't my link to the convention, I'd be worried that I was slipping.

But I trusted Juan, despite our many disagreements (don't get us started on Clinton's bombing of Serbia). Juan accepts me for who I am—or, rather, such as I am.

YearlyKos, partisan product of Markos Moulitsas, a big libblogging daddy and hustler for the Democrats, convened in Chicago's Hyatt McCormick in August, 2007. It was the second annual gathering of online liberals who fancied themselves "netroots" activists, changing the American political scene one keystroke at a time. Throughout the two days I was there, I heard about the power and influence of libblogging from various people, some of whom seemed seriously to believe in it. But then, that's what conventions are all about: the likeminded rubbing shoulders while strengthening a collective identity.

When I first arrived in the hotel's lobby, I immediately spotted several Kossacks, identifiable by the large plastic badges hanging around their necks. As I strolled along, more and more bloggers appeared, many of whom were sitting on the floor, tapping away at their laptops. Then, as if on cue, Kos himself emerged from the crowd, elfin grin on his small face. When we crossed paths, Kos looked directly at me and smiled, nodding hello. I'm certain he had no idea who I was, for if he had I doubt he'd have been as jovial. In any event, Kos looked pleased, and why not? His little political empire was expanding, and the bustle of bloggers tapping and chatting under his name must have been sweet music to his ears.

After walking for what seemed like carpeted miles, I found the registration area and went to formalize my arrival. The woman at the counter confirmed my place on the afternoon panel, gave me my personal plastic badge, along with a YearlyKos tote bag filled with all kinds of crap. Now I was part of the scene, though I immediately noticed a blue ribbon adorning my badge that read "Speaker." Looking around, I saw different colored ribbons on various badges. Orange was for attendees, bloggers who were not on panels. Green was for the media. And, naturally, blue was for we "experts" who would shed light and wisdom from our various perches.

I was pissed off and dismayed. Why the fuck were there color-coded distinctions at a supposedly "democratic" convention? I thought the whole point to blogging was to democratize political expression, to allow people who didn't attend an Ivy League school or have friends in the corporate media to reach a wide audience with their views and concerns. But at YearlyKos, we were immediately categorized. A hierarchy of sorts was established, and this was reinforced when I dropped in on the "Blogs and the MSM: From Clash to Civilization" panel taking place in the big ballroom.

On stage sat Jay Carney of *Time*, Jill Filipovic of Feministe, Mike Allen of Politico (and formerly of *Time*), and Glenn Greenwald of Salon. The *Nation*'s Ari Melber moderated. In order to enhance the panel's importance, their images were magnified to Oz-like proportions on large screens flanking their table. When I walked in,

Greenwald was droning on about responsible media, the duty of journalists in a democracy, or some such shit. It was the same tired, clichéd pap I've heard at practically every mainstream media panel I've ever attended. And here it was again, only presented in "cutting edge" wrapping. Nothing about the corporate structure of "news" and how that limits and distorts actual journalism, unless they tackled this before I showed up. But given the remarks made in my presence, I seriously doubt that topic was ever broached.

There were two lines of questioners at microphones in the audience, and it was clear that Melber wanted to move things along at a swift pace. Now, I understand that, as a moderator, you don't want a questioner to give a speech. It takes up time and limits the access of others. I get that, having been in the same position myself. But there appeared to be some hostility to those bloggers on the floor who had critical things to say. After all, if their opinions mattered, they'd be on the panel, right? Of course, if one praised the panel for its insight and journalistic courage, no question was required for speaking rights. Hail the experts, and you can talk all day.

I'd seen enough, and went to check into my room to prepare for my panel.

I rifled through the tote bag given to me downstairs. It was filled mostly with Dem party hand-outs, the latest issue of the *Nation*, and a few knick-knacks like a ONE bracelet that promoted an anti-poverty activist group. I slipped that on in the spirit of camaraderie, then read some of the hand-outs. The bigger bloggers and various Dem Congresspeople attending the convention were referred to as "our netroots heroes," once again reinforcing the We-and-You concept. Far from breaking down elitist walls, YearlyKos was adding a large wing to their media mansion. Bow down, you simple bloggers from the boonies, and honor your online superiors. It's the "progressive" thing to do.

As I went through my satchel to gather some notes, the small, compact joint I'd packed fell out. Temptation. Would it be wise to have a little taste before mixing again with liberal blogland? From what I had already seen, this was a very straight-laced affair, mostly white, quiet, professional. Heightening my awareness—or worse, flirting with full psychoactive immersion—could prove too much. I'm not the young risk-taker I once was, someone who'd enter the most chaotic environment with a head sizzling with chemicals. YearlyKos was the opposite of chaos—machine-driven, semi-robotic, technocratic and corporate-friendly. Wandering through that scene after kissing the green tit might push me over the edge and send me to the hotel bar for liquid balance. That wouldn't bode well for my talk, however fractured and entertaining my performance.

So, completely sober, I went downstairs to tour more of the convention, blue ribbon badge around my neck. I felt out of place, and wondered if any of these bloggers read my stuff. I received a few nods and smiles from those who saw my name, but I think that had more to do with my being an "expert" than with any knowledge of who I was and what I wrote. Indeed, a few people I talked to knew nothing of my blog; but when I said I was on a panel with Juan Cole, their eyes lit up. "Juan Cole is awesome! You know him?!"

Not long after this, Juan himself appeared, alongside his wife, Shahin. We greeted each other and began to make our way to our panel, when we came upon Sidney and Max Blumenthal—two generations of Dem royalty who were walking in the opposite direction with Sidney's sister and I believe his wife, though I wasn't really sure since we weren't formally introduced. Max made a beeline for Juan, shaking his hand and telling him how much he loved Juan's work. Juan then introduced me to Max, who shook my hand with a brief, "Oh, hi," before turning his full attention to Juan. Max's aunt introduced herself, and she noticed that I was staring at her large Hillary Clinton button.

"Do you like Hillary?" she asked.

"No, not really."

"Why not?"

"It's probably best not to go into it here." I didn't

want to start a conversation about how much I dislike
the Dems with someone from the Blumenthal clan,
especially right before I was due to speak.

"Well, who do you like?"

"Actually, I'd like to see another system, to be honest."

"Well, that's not gonna happen."

Not with people like you in the way, I thought to
myself.

"Give me one name. Just one."

"If you insist, I'll go with Dennis Kucinich."

"Ewww." Her face scrunched, then widened. "He does
have a beautiful wife, however."

Sidney stepped forward to shake hands and introduce
himself. He was pleasant but stiff, skin like polished
naugahyde. We chatted very briefly before Juan told
everyone that we had a panel to attend. We said our
goodbyes and parted, but I couldn't help watching the
Blumenthals as they walked regally away. They are real
celebrities within Dem circles, and I would later see Max
constantly fawned over by young, white, male liberals like
himself. He clearly enjoyed their veneration.

In contrast, our panel seemed pushed to the side, an
afterthought to the grander Kos stages. Our room was in
the furthest corner of the bottom floor. The panel before
us bled into our time, forcing us to start late. Then we
discovered we had no moderator, so Juan assumed that
role, and he and I bussed the panel table, clearing away

used water cups and coffee containers. There was no fresh water for us; we had to make do with what was left over from the previous panel. It was a disheveled start, but the audience quickly filed in and filled up the seats, with more standing in the back and to the side. Once things settled down, Juan welcomed everyone, and the panel kicked off, with us speaking in alphabetical order.

Manan Ahmed, a professor at the University of Chicago, got the party started with a detailed critique of Barack Obama's then recent statements about possibly bombing Pakistan. Manan gave a meticulous PowerPoint presentation illustrating just how craven and idiotic Obama's remarks were. Unlike the fantasy Pakistan that Obama depicted, where President Pervez Musharraf was dragging his heels on fighting extremism, and it might take US air strikes to focus his attention, the Pakistani army was battling extremists in the North Waziristan region—fighting that was comparable to combat in Iraq. Also, the US had already hit Pakistan, on November 10, 2006, shelling a madrassa in Bajaur, which resulted in zero al-Qaeda dead, but did manage to kill some of the seminary's children.

Manan made those in the audience wearing Obama buttons shift a bit in their seats and look down to the floor. I thought there might be some audible disagreement from them, given that we were on Dem party turf, and Obama love was all over the Kos convention. But they said nothing. Manan so thoroughly dismantled Obama's speech that his supporters had no real comeback to it. I doubt they know much more about Pakistan than did their hero; but after Manan's talk, they might have absorbed a general idea. Sometimes learning can be a painful experience, but in the end we're all winners.

Juan took the podium next, and gave a very animated, at times funny, talk about the possible future for Iraq. Juan insisted—and I largely disagreed with him—that US troops would be withdrawn by 2009 at the latest, leaving Iraq to whatever fate then befell it. In Juan's view, the Sunnis, after a bloodbath, would once again control Baghdad, and a new Baath Party would most likely be created. The Shias would retreat to the south, and the Kurds would go about their business in the north, ready to fight should the Sunnis attempt any incursion on their turf. In other words, Iraq would roughly be what it more or less was after the first Gulf War—minus Saddam and his sons, of course.

John Mearsheimer, also from the University of Chicago, followed Juan, and his presentation, about the four possible roads Israel might take with regard to the Palestinians, was extremely sensible, to the point of being predictable. John had received acres of abuse since his and Stephen Walt's paper on the Israeli lobby had been released. But in person John was a very polite, friendly, down-to-earth guy. You'd half expect to meet a fire-breathing Jew-hater, given some of the attacks he had endured; but, as is usually the case in this area, the sliming has little-to-nothing to do with the actual person. If anything, John was too cautious and conservative. When he said that, of the remaining options left to Israel, the most likely one would be some form of apartheid for the Palestinians, I wanted to interrupt him by saying that this had pretty much already happened. But I'm a team player when it comes to panels, and besides, it might come up during Q&A.

Finally, me. As I grabbed the podium mike, I said that following three distinguished academics with my more showbiz background left me with only one way to greet the crowd: "Yo yo yo, YearlyKos, whazzzz upppp!" This got a nice laugh, which I built on by quoting Condi Rice's statement from Ramallah, as reported by one of my favorite comedy sources, the *New York Times*: "'We believe strongly in the right of people to express themselves and their desires in elections.' But, [Rice] added, once elected, 'you have the obligation to govern responsibly.'" An even bigger laugh. In comedy, found humor is often your best friend.

I then delivered the crux of my talk, which I truncated a bit due to time constraints. Essentially, I made two points: 1) Unlike the Vietnam era, where there had been an abundance of antiwar satire and comedy, from the *National Lampoon* to The Committee to The Smothers Brothers (among others), the Iraq era had been satirically deficient, save for a few exceptions like the *Daily Show*, which wasn't all that cutting, given the horror that surrounded us; and 2) You could not find mainstream American comics and comedy shows that skewer Israelis and Zionists with the same nasty, at times openly racist, routines that were commonly employed against Arabs and Muslims. Judaism and Jewish culture had been sent up by Jewish comics since vaudeville. But where, I asked the audience, did you see satirical assaults on Israeli Zionists?

No one answered, for the simple reason that this kind of comedy scarcely exists. The *Onion* has done a few funny bits about Israeli aggression, but try getting that on the *Daily Show*, much less *Saturday Night Live*, Jay Leno, David Letterman, or Conan O'Brien.

The Q&A focused mostly on Israel/Palestine, with some bantering about the future of Iraq. Pakistan and Obama did not come up, for obvious reasons, and after a while Juan specifically asked the crowd for a Pakistan question so that Manan could be part of the discussion. One was asked, Manan thoughtfully responded, then it was back to the war and the Israelis and Palestinians.

At one point, both Juan and John agreed that there was no significant counterweight in American politics to that of groups like AIPAC. An older woman from the back began yelling, "That's not true! That's not true!" Since our panel was not afforded mike stands in the audience, Juan invited the woman to take the podium and explain herself. She ran down the aisle as the rest of the crowd applauded her. She gave an impassioned speech about how, being Jewish, what Israel was ostensibly doing in her name appalled and saddened her. She said she was part of a Jewish peace group, Brit Tzedek v'Shalom, and that they were doing all they could to counter the effects of AIPAC. Another member in the audience added to this, but said that the main problem was money. No one on the panel wanted to rub in the obvious fact that this group had no realistic shot at diminishing AIPAC's political influence, at least not at that point; and the woman, after engaging a few more people in the audience, eventually went back to her seat.

I thought Juan's invitation to the woman was very democratic—very unlike the rest of YearlyKos, at least when it came to "expert" panels. Our audience was very opinionated and energetic, but before long Juan shut the whole thing down, noting that we were going overtime. I felt that, since we were the last panel, we should have kept going for at least another half-hour. But once Juan had made his announcement, the majority of people left, with a few hanging on, sharing with me their favorite comedy bits.

A few hours later, back in my room, I finally took a few sharp hits from the joint, blowing the smoke through the bathroom vent so as not to set off the detector. Then a nice hot shower, a change of clothes, and downstairs to a party organized by Laughing Liberally, a collection of supposedly funny liberals. Having been exposed to a few comics in my time, I was curious to see what passed for humor among these young Democrats—though the allure of an open bar added to my interest.

Perhaps it was age, but the party seemed more like a college dorm bash than drinks at the Algonquin. The noise was such that a person's joke or observation had to be shouted, and sometimes repeated, to be somewhat understood. That didn't help matters. But worse was the fact that the material essentially stunk. There was no budding Bill Hicks in that room. And this is what pissed me off more than anything about YearlyKos: the lack of genuine anger about the American imperial system.

Here we were, ostensible progressives from around the nation, and the only real passion shown was a desire to find a Democratic presidential candidate who would deliver us all from Bush/Cheney evil. When major mules like Hillary Clinton and Barack Obama appeared at the convention, there was no agitation, only excitement— the kind you see when teenagers get near their favorite bands. The fixed American electoral system wasn't a major issue. The global wars were an abstraction; corporate rule taken as a given. Not even the comedians drew blood, preferring to be light, diverting, amusing. By the time hotel security broke up the party, which had spilled into the hallway, I was bored and dismayed. I filled a glass with vodka and ice, grabbed two Heinekens, and slunk back to my room, getting mildly drunk while watching a later-season *Seinfeld*, when the show had ceased to be funny, the principals just cashing their checks. Appropriate entertainment for that evening.

I won't say that all of the YearlyKossacks were deluded. Despite their general conformity concerning the Democrats, we are talking about a diverse group of people and different levels of awareness. Still, there was the air that somehow, some way, libloggers were making a difference—perhaps not a large difference; but that some kind of online momentum was building to 2008 and beyond. I'm sure there's some truth to this. The top presidential candidates came to court them, after all. But in the larger picture, liberals who blog on behalf of Dems are a sweat drop in the big corporate tank. They help with the Party's propaganda, maybe flog a serious issue here and there, but that's about it. Meanwhile the corporate gravy-train plows right over them on its way to finance Hillary, Obama, or whoever big business thinks can advance its private interests.

Indeed, if anything was missing at YearlyKos, it was anti-corporate agitation and awareness. Which is not surprising, given that the major liberal blogs rarely go after the companies that help keep their beloved Party solvent. For without those big bucks and the various interests tied to them, the Democrats pretty much cease to exist. Fine by me, but sadly, that's not going to happen in my lifetime. The Dem elites will continue to gorge on corporate money and favors, assuming, quite correctly, that most of their voting base will look past this piggery in the hope that some crumbs will fall to the ground.

About the harshest criticism libloggers will toss at their rulers is that the Dems have no spine, or simply capitulate to GOP wishes without really knowing what's at stake. I heard this from several people at YearlyKos when word of the FISA vote spread around. "What's wrong with them? Don't they get it?" Oh, they get it all right. They understand exactly what they're doing. They wouldn't be in the position to authorize expansive, domestic wire-tapping if they didn't "get it." The Dems have a spine: it simply curves rightward when the imperial state needs bolstering.

When faced with this stark reality, libloggers avert their eyes and pretend that the Dems suffer from some weird personality defect—that they're easily swayed or intimidated. This soft-focus projection has got to be better than dealing with the harsh facts of corporate capitalism and privatized state power.

You wouldn't know how deeply buried in corpse-choked shit we are, rattling about in our respective crates, looking for any distraction from the slaughterhouse on the hill. Liberals are anxiously dreaming, insisting that it's their birthright to have a Democratic president elected in

2008, and that when that happens the universe will begin to right itself. At least, they hope that's the case. Contemporary American liberalism is all about hope. They turn their sad mule eyes to their keepers, trusting that the blades being sharpened aren't intended for their throats.

Little wonder that Barack Obama's rhetoric cast such a strong, hypnotic spell over them. His oratory was sweet music among the crates—heavy heads bobbing to the beat. Hillary simply spooked the room, putting everyone on edge, even though, if it came down to it, the powerless mules would take her over any GOP keeper. But Saint Obama spun much gentler yarns, elevating captive moods while keeping all in place. After the madness of the Bush years, Obama clearly seemed the most logical choice to manage the abattoir—smiling, waving, oiling his hammer gun, making sure that the conveyor belt's running smoothly and efficiently.

What do mules dream about as they await the abattoir blades? Hopefully, something pleasant and soothing. In the mule crate, all you have are your dreams.